THOMAS JEFFERSON

PRESIDENTIAL ✧ LEADERS

THOMAS JEFFERSON

CAROL H. BEHRMAN

⌐ LERNER PUBLICATIONS COMPANY/MINNEAPOLIS

This book about a great American is dedicated to my beloved
children—Bonnie, Joe, and Linda.

Lerner Publications Company
A division of Lerner Publishing Group
241 First Avenue North
Minneapolis, MN 55401 U.S.A.

Website address: www.lernerbooks.com

Library of Congress Cataloging-in-Publication Data

Behrman, Carol H.
    Thomas Jefferson / by Carol H. Behrman.
        p.   cm. — (Presidential leaders)
    Summary: A biography of Thomas Jefferson—patriot, president, and author of the
Declaration of Independence. Includes bibliographical references and index.
    ISBN: 0–8225–0822–2 (lib.bdg. : alk. paper)
    1. Jefferson, Thomas, 1743–1826—Juvenile literature. 2. Presidents, United States—
Biography—Juvenile literature. [1. Jefferson, Thomas, 1743–1826. 2. Presidents.] I. Title.
II. Series.
    E332.79.B44 2004
    973.4'6'092—dc22   2003014495

Manufactured in the United States of America
1 2 3 4 5 6 – JR – 09 08 07 06 05 04

CONTENTS

Jefferson (right) spent many hours drafting the Declaration of Independence. This painting shows him reading his first draft to Benjamin Franklin (left).

INTRODUCTION

*"Whenever any form of Government
becomes destructive . . . , it is the right
of the people to alter or abolish it."*
—The Declaration of Independence, 1776

The red-haired young man sat hunched over a desk in his second-floor room. The chair and desk were small for his tall, lanky frame, but he was too absorbed in his task to notice. His pen moved across the page, trying to keep up with thoughts taking shape in his mind. He scratched out words and phrases as better ones occurred to him.

Every so often, he would get up to stretch. Walking over to the window, he could see the bustle of city activity below. It was very different from his own isolated home on a mountaintop. He listened to the clip-clop of horses' hooves and the clatter of carriage wheels on the cobblestoned street. He watched the inhabitants of the city moving briskly about their business. He knew that his friends, John Adams and Ben Franklin, were somewhere nearby. They were probably deep in conversation at this very moment worrying about how he was getting on. But they would not disturb him. The task in which he was engaged was too important to them, to him, and to their fellow patriots.

He returned to his work, picked up the quill pen, and dipped it in the inkpot. When he finished, he would hold in his hand one of the most influential documents ever written. Its impassioned words for freedom and human rights would ring like a bell of liberty throughout the world and change the course of history.

The year was 1776, the place, Philadelphia. The man's name was Thomas Jefferson. The revolutionary words he was writing became the Declaration of Independence.

CHAPTER ONE

A BOYHOOD
ON THE PLANTATION

"My father was the third or fourth settler,
about the year 1737, of the part
of the country in which I live."
—Thomas Jefferson

Thomas Jefferson was born on April 13, 1743. His mother, Jane, was a Randolph, from one of the most important families in Virginia. His father, Peter, was a self-made man. Through hard work and intelligence, Peter Jefferson had built a large tobacco plantation in the Piedmont section of Virginia near the Blue Ridge Mountains. He called it Shadwell after the town in England where his wife's mother had been born. With the help of slave labor, Peter became wealthy growing tobacco. The tobacco was stored in sturdy barrels, called hogsheads. It was shipped by wagon or by double canoes (two canoes lashed together) down the narrow Rivanna

River to the James River. There it could be loaded onto large, oceangoing vessels for shipment to England.

Peter Jefferson was admired in Virginia as an explorer and surveyor. He braved the dangers of the wilderness to map out large portions of the territory. On one perilous expedition, he and his group were attacked during the day by wild animals. At night they had to sleep high in the trees to keep safe. They ran out of food and supplies and had to survive by their wits. Together with another explorer, Peter Jefferson surveyed and drew up the first complete map of Virginia. He was also famous throughout the area for his extraordinary physical strength. He could lift two hogsheads of tobacco, weighing one thousand pounds each, according to Henry Randall, an early biographer.

At the time Thomas Jefferson was born, Virginia was one of thirteen American colonies ruled by Great Britain. Peter Jefferson was a member of the Virginia House of Burgesses, which was responsible for making laws for the colony under the British royal governor. He was appointed a colonel of the militia, a group of part-time volunteer soldiers, and given the job of keeping order on the frontier. He did this by becoming friends with Native Americans from that area and offering them the hospitality of his house. A Cherokee chief, Ontassete, was a friend to Peter and his son, Tom. In a letter to John Adams, Tom later wrote about having visited Ontassete. "His voice . . . and the solemn silence of the people at their [camp] fires filled me with awe." As a boy, Tom loved to explore abandoned Indian villages and collect arrowheads. Later, he often supported the rights of Native Americans.

Even though the plantation was immense and isolated,

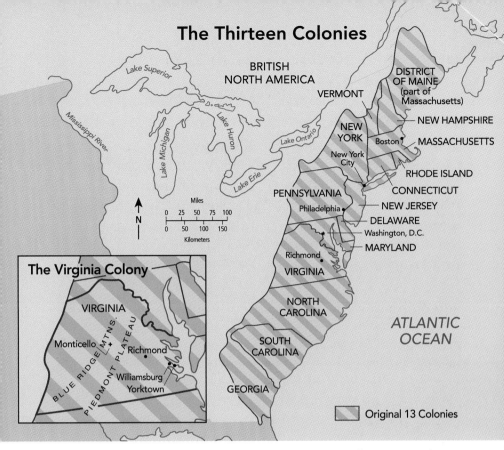

The thirteen American colonies were under British rule when Tom was born.

Tom never felt lonely. The Jefferson family was fun loving and continued to grow.

When Tom was two, a relative and close friend named William Randolph died. Before he died, he had begged Peter Jefferson to become his son's guardian and to take care of his plantation and three orphaned children. It was impossible to do this from a distance, and Shadwell was not big enough for such a large, combined family. In 1745 Peter moved his family from Shadwell to the larger Randolph plantation. Peter Jefferson's only payment for uprooting his wife and children was the knowledge that he was keeping a promise to a dying friend.

Tom spent much of his childhood at Shadwell.
He enjoyed wandering across its vast acres.

———————————— ✧ ————————————

Tom always remembered how a servant carried him on horseback atop a pillow along wilderness trails to the Randolph estate. Tuckahoe was much more splendid than Shadwell. At the estate, the Jefferson children played with the young Randolphs. They were taught by private tutors and given dancing lessons in Tuckahoe's grand salon under a gleaming crystal chandelier.

Tom had two older sisters, Jane and Mary, and three younger ones, Elizabeth, Martha, and Lucy. Later, the twins, Anna and Randolph, came along. Peter Jefferson gave a lot of attention to his first-born son. Young Tom worshiped his father and dreamed of becoming a surveyor and explorer just like him.

The Jefferson family remained at Tuckahoe for seven years, until the Randolph children were old enough to be on their own. When they returned home, Tom, who was nine years old, continued his idyllic childhood at Shadwell. He played up and down the forested hills and along the Rivanna River, which curved like a snake through the plantation. His sister Jane, who was three years older, often accompanied him. "I duly acknowledge," he later wrote, "that I have gone through a long life, with fewer . . . afflictions than . . . most men."

From an early age, Tom was made to feel a sense of responsibility in return for his privileged life. His mother and father emphasized the importance of education. Peter Jefferson wanted his son to be strong physically and mentally. He taught him to love outdoor sports, to hunt, fish, swim, and ride horseback. He insisted that Tom learn the practical skills required on a plantation. Tom was taught how to make a round barrel out of pieces of wood, churn

Slaves labored on the Jefferson plantation, where Tom's father wanted him to learn the value of hard work.

cream into butter, and separate healthy tobacco leaves from poor ones. He learned the value of rotating crops to keep the soil fertile by planting tobacco in a field one year and corn the next.

BOARDING SCHOOL

By the time he was six, Tom had read most of the books in his father's library. At the age of nine, he was sent to study and board with the Reverend William Douglas in Northam, fifty miles from home. Tom's father gave him a beautiful leather-bound Latin dictionary as a going-away gift.

Tom did not like the stern, cold-mannered Douglas. He was even less fond of Mrs. Douglas's bad-tasting, moldy pies. He studied hard, learning Greek, Latin, and French. He even memorized the rules of "manners" that gentlemen were required to know, such as "Spit not, cough not, nor blow thy nose at table." All the while, Tom looked forward to the long, wonderful summers at Shadwell. There he was free to hunt, fish, and canoe with friends and roam the hillsides with his sister Jane. During their walks, they often stood upon a ridge and admired a beautiful mountaintop about a mile distant. Tom thought how wonderful it would be if he could some day live on this mountain.

When Tom was fourteen, his happy, carefree world fell apart. In the summer of 1757, Peter Jefferson was stricken with a mysterious infection. The doctors had no cure for the illness. Tom's strong father seemed as indestructible as the Virginia hills, but his condition quickly worsened. On August 17, he died.

Peter Jefferson had been Tom's hero. His most cherished goal had been to grow up to be just like his father. He had dreamed of them exploring the wilderness side by side. But with his father gone, that could never happen. Tom had two consolations in this time of grief. The first was that his father left him the things he valued most: his surveying implements, his cherry wood writing desk, and his library of forty books.

Second, Peter Jefferson's dying words had been about his son. He instructed his wife to make sure that Tom's schooling continue and that he should receive a thorough classical education. Thomas Jefferson later said he was grateful to his father for all he had done for him, but the opportunity to become educated was the greatest gift of all.

CHAPTER TWO

THE SCHOLAR

"When I recollect that at 14 years of age the
whole care and direction of myself was thrown
on my self entirely, without a relative or friend
qualified to advise or guide me . . . I am
astonished I did not become worthless."
—Thomas Jefferson

Thomas Jefferson never forgot the agony and confusion his father's death brought. It was not only his own care that was thrust upon Tom. As the eldest son, he felt responsible for the whole family, including his mother, six sisters, and one brother. His father's will divided the estate between Tom and his brother, Randolph. Tom inherited the property containing the house where he had been born. Tom's sisters were provided for, and Mrs. Jefferson was given the use of the house and farm for the rest of her life.

Since the children would not inherit until the age of twenty-one, Peter Jefferson appointed five honest men as guardians to advise Mrs. Jefferson and the children. In this way, responsibility for the family's welfare was lifted from Tom's young shoulders. He was free to follow his father's dying wish for him to continue his education. The first decision he made on his own was to change schools. Douglas's curriculum was limited. Tom decided to study with the Reverend Dr. Joseph Maury, only fourteen miles from Shadwell.

Maury was a classical scholar and had far more to offer than   Douglas. He taught Tom to be proficient in Latin, Greek, French, and Italian. Maury had a library of four hundred books. It was a feast for the young scholar. He spent many hours poring over these volumes and taking notes. He practiced the violin three hours a day. Tom made friends with other students too. One of these was Dabney Carr, who was his closest friend all through school, college, and beyond.

One of the best things about Maury's school was its closeness to Shadwell. Tom was able to go home

—————————— ✧

One of Tom's favorite activities was playing his violin, which was similar to this one.

for the weekends. Often Carr came with him. They studied together and hiked through the woods and fields to the hill called Little Mountain. There, Tom and Dabney made a pact. They solemnly promised that if one died, the other would bury him beneath the spreading oak tree where they stood.

Tom and his sister Jane became even closer. They shared many of the same interests—reading, walking, and discussing every topic under the sun. They were both passionate about music. Jane often sang in her sweet, pure voice while Tom accompanied her on the violin.

After two years of instruction, Maury and Tom agreed that he was ready for college. First, Tom had to convince his guardians. He wrote them a letter expressing his wish to attend William and Mary College in Williamsburg, Virginia. "By going to college," he wrote, "I shall get a more universal acquaintance which may . . . be serviceable to me. I can pursue my studies in Greek and Latin . . . and likewise learn something of Mathematics."

The guardians agreed. In the spring of 1760, Tom rode off to Williamsburg. He was not quite seventeen years old.

COLLEGE YEARS

Williamsburg was the capital of the Virginia Colony and a center of political, social, and intellectual activity. It was a small, picturesque city with a main street more than one mile long. At one end was the Capitol building. William and Mary College, a respected center of learning, stood at the other. The imposing brick building was already sixty-six years old when Thomas Jefferson arrived.

Tom settled into college life as easily as a groundhog into its burrow. College rules were strict. No racehorses were

Tom immediately took to college life at William and Mary. He was an eager student and absorbed as much knowledge as he could.

————————— ✧ —————————

allowed on campus. There was to be no gambling, lying, cursing, or fighting. Fortunately for students, these rules were seldom enforced. The city of Williamsburg offered many opportunities for pleasure. There were horse racing at the track and performances of plays at a new theater on Waller Street. The Raleigh Tavern was a popular gathering spot. Balls were held in its Apollo Room. Tom Jefferson could be found among the young folks dancing minuets and the Virginia reel. He was tall, gangling, and freckled. Though a bit shy, his intelligent hazel-blue eyes, clever conversation, and charming manners made him a favorite among the ladies as well as with his fellow students. He might have found himself drawn into so many activities that he neglected his studies, but he was fortunate enough to meet some extraordinary companions.

A professor of mathematics, Dr. William Small, befriended Tom. Small was more than just a mathematician. He was an outstanding scholar, a deep thinker, and a philosopher, who introduced his students to exciting new ideas. He taught them to use reason and the new scientific method—observation and experimentation—to solve problems. In his memoirs, Thomas Jefferson describes Small as "a man profound in . . . science with . . . an enlarged and liberal mind . . . [who]made me his daily companion." He goes on to write that having Small as his mentor "probably fixed the destinies of my life." Tom was fascinated with the new scientific method. He was eager to use this exciting knowledge in practical ways. On vacations at Shadwell, he figured out a better way to rotate the crops. He also invented a new kind of plow.

William Small recognized that the redheaded youth had unusual ability. He introduced Tom to two other men who had a strong influence upon his development. One was

———————————————— ◇ ————————————————

Jefferson's mind was never at rest. This diagram of a plow shows just one of his inventions.

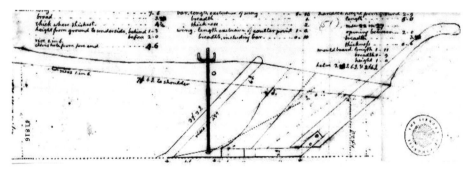

George Wythe, a brilliant lawyer. Jefferson called Wythe a "faithful and beloved mentor in youth . . . and my most affectionate friend through life." He added that Wythe was "devoted . . . to liberty and the natural and equal rights of man." The other was the royal governor of Virginia, Francis Fauquier. According to Jefferson, Fauquier was "the ablest man ever to hold that office." These four—the gifted scholar, the great lawyer, the worldly governor, and the young student—spent many hours together. The older men saw something in the precocious young man that made him a desirable companion. For Tom, it was an opportunity to mingle with great men and to absorb their knowledge. The dinner-table discussions Tom shared with these learned men contained "more good sense, more rational and philosophical conversation than in all my life," he wrote. These companions set Tom upon the course he would follow in life. "In a moment of temptation or difficulty," he wrote, "I would ask myself, 'What would Dr. Small, Mr. Wythe . . . do in this situation[?]'"

Tom burned with a desire for knowledge. He learned calculus, physics, natural science, astronomy, agriculture, history, and languages. He studied fifteen hours a day,

George Wythe

———— ✧ ————

poring over his books until 2 A.M. Then he rose with the first dim rays of dawn to begin again.

Tom found time to enjoy acquaintances his own age. Dabney Carr followed him to William and Mary. He also became friends with John Tyler, another hardworking student. He continued to be a favorite with the girls. While at college, Thomas Jefferson fell in love for the first time. The girl's name was Rebecca Burwell. She was beautiful, popular, and flirtatious. Tom poured out his feelings about Rebecca in letters to his friend Dabney Carr. He wrote love poems that were never sent. Rebecca married someone else, and Tom's first romance was over before it really began.

The college years flew by in a flurry of intellectual excitement. In 1762 Tom finished his studies at William and Mary. At nineteen he found himself at a crossroads. He could go home and live the life of a gentleman planter. Tom loved Shadwell. He had an intense attachment to the land on which he had been raised. On the other hand, he wanted to accomplish something greater in the world beyond his own farm.

CHAPTER THREE

THE YOUNG LAWYER

"He always took the right side."
—a courtroom observer, describing Jefferson
as a young Virginia lawyer

Tom Jefferson had acquired many skills by the time he graduated from the College of William and Mary in 1762. He was fluent in Greek, Latin, French, and Italian. He had read the works of ancient and modern philosophers in their own languages. He was knowledgeable about all the sciences. Thanks to his three mentors and his own hard work, nineteen-year old Tom Jefferson was one of the best-educated men in Virginia.

Jefferson's friends, Dabney Carr and John Tyler, had decided to study law. Patrick Henry, another friend, was doing the same. Jefferson thought that law would be an interesting profession. At that time, there were no law schools in the colonies. A young man became a lawyer by studying with a licensed attorney. Jefferson already knew someone who fit that description. George Wythe was delighted to take on his young friend as an apprentice. Wythe was considered the best teacher of law in Virginia. He had one of the largest law practices in the colony. "In the learning of the law," it was said, "he stood . . . almost alone." Many of Wythe's students later became outstanding leaders. His favorite was always Jefferson. When Wythe died years later, the old lawyer left all his books to Jefferson.

Jefferson benefited from the older man's experience and knowledge of the law. Wythe was fascinated by his student's determination to know everything. Jefferson believed he could understand the laws of his day by studying those of the past. He pored over volumes of legal history back to ancient Roman and Greek times. Jefferson even learned to read old English laws in their original form. He wrote down everything in a notebook that he called his *Commonplace Book.* This was one of many such notebooks that

This page is from one of Jefferson's legal Commonplace Books. He kept many such notebooks through the years.

Jefferson would keep, where he carefully recorded every aspect of life ranging from the cost of nails to complex architectural plans.

Jefferson had to stay in Williamsburg in order to study with Wythe. He continued to meet with his other mentors, Small and Fauquier, and shared rooms with fellow law student John Tyler. In addition to his law studies, Jefferson observed the stars and recorded weather activity. He practiced the violin daily. With his friends, he went out to dances, dinners, and the theater. He attended court proceedings as part of his training and made extensive notes in his *Commonplace Book* about everything he observed.

Jefferson studied with Wythe for five years. During that time, he turned twenty-one and became responsible for the management of Shadwell. He returned home often to supervise the work on the plantation. Jefferson loved his native soil and constantly tried to improve it. On his twenty-first birthday in 1764, he planted an avenue of locust trees at the estate. He returned to his early dream of building a house atop Little Mountain. He taught himself to become expert in all forms of architecture so that he would be able to design his perfect home.

Carr often went along on Jefferson's journeys to Shadwell. They tramped over the hills and valleys and canoed across the river. They spent endless hours discussing law, philosophy, and literature. Their friendship deepened year by year.

During these visits to Shadwell, Carr grew to know the Jefferson family well. He was fond of them all. For one in particular, his feelings became more than friendship. Carr fell in love with his friend's younger sister Martha. Martha returned his affection, and they were married at Shadwell in July 1765. Jefferson and his sister Jane stood up for the young couple. Jefferson and Carr were not only best friends, but also brothers-in-law. A few years later, Jefferson described Carr after his marriage in a letter. "In a very small house, with a table, half a dozen chairs . . . the happiest man in the universe."

A GRIEVOUS LOSS

Jefferson returned to Williamsburg after the wedding. A week later, his joy turned to sorrow. A message arrived telling him that his beloved older sister, Jane, had fallen ill and died. She was twenty-five years old. Jane was the sister he was closest to. She was his companion and fellow maker of music. To her, he had confided his deepest thoughts and desires. Later, when he was planning his hilltop home, he built a family cemetery and had Jane's body transferred there. He tried to make the spot as beautiful as possible for her. "Choose out for a Burying place," he instructed, "some . . . vale [valley] in the park where is no sound to break the stillness but a brook . . . bubbling among the weeds. . . . In the center of it, erect a small Gothic temple . . . (and) an altar."

Jane had always loved flowers. Soon after her death, Jefferson began to plant and raise flowers. He kept a "Garden Book" where he noted their progress. The first entry was "Purple hyacinth begins to bloom." In this journal, he kept a record of the flowering and death of every blossom in his garden as a memorial to his sister. Jefferson's grandchildren reported that even in old age he still spoke about Jane "in terms of as warm admiration and love as if the grave had but just closed over her."

Grieving over the loss of Jane, Jefferson returned to Williamsburg and his law books. In 1767, two years after his sister's death, he completed his studies and was admitted to the Virginia bar. He was advised to set up a practice in Williamsburg near the courts, but the only home Jefferson wanted was his farm. "Those who labour in the earth," he wrote, "are the chosen people of God." He returned to his plans for his ideal house on Little Mountain. He read books on Italian architecture. Gradually, his vision for a home became clear. He began to draw plans for a classic manor complete with beautiful gardens and orchards. Jefferson called the house Monticello, meaning "little mountain" in Italian. Even before building started, he was busy experimenting with different varieties of flowers and trees. His "Garden Book" entries for 1767 contain the first mention of his house's name. "Inoculated common cherry buds . . . at Monticello."

Little Mountain was only four miles from Shadwell. Jefferson needed to be near his family. He was responsible for his mother and the four children still at home. These included three young children and his twenty-one-year-old sister, Elizabeth, who was developmentally challenged and needed special care until her death at the age of thirty.

THE TRAVELING LAWYER

It was costly to run a plantation and take care of a large family. Jefferson had to earn an income through his law practice. During the next eight years, he handled almost one thousand cases and became a respected attorney. He

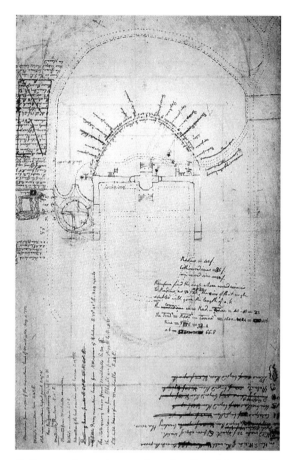

Jefferson planned every last detail at Monticello.
This diagram shows Jefferson's plans for the
plants to include in the garden.

——————— ✧ ———————

developed one of the largest legal practices in Virginia, riding about two hundred miles a month visiting clients and
courts around the colony.

One of Jefferson's best-known cases involved a slave
named Samuel Howell. Slavery was legal and common in

Virginia. Howell claimed he had the right to freedom because his great-grandmother had been a free white woman. Tom knew that Howell could not pay him, and he was sure to lose the case. He took it on because he felt it was the right thing to do. He argued that under the law of nature, all people are born free. The judge was shocked and angry. He ruled against Howell, but the case had given Thomas Jefferson his first opportunity to express his ideas about freedom and liberty.

When he was twenty-five, Jefferson was elected to the Virginia House of Burgesses. He was proud to be following in the footsteps of his father, who had also served in this lawmaking group. Jefferson immediately used his position to oppose slavery. Slave owners in Virginia were not allowed to

─────────────────── ✧ ───────────────────

After his unsuccessful attempt to win freedom, Jefferson's client Howell ran away with his brother. Their owner placed this ad in the Virginia Gazette, *offering a reward for their return.*

R UN away from the subscriber, in *Cumberland* county, two mulatto servant men. SAMUEL HOWELL, about 28 years old, well set, about 5 feet 8 or 9 inches high; he is a sensible fellow and a good sawer. SIMON HOWELL, brother to *Samuel*, about 25 years of age, 5 feet 8 or 9 inches high, has a thin visage, and sharp chin. They went off in their common labouring dress, and took no other clothes with them that I can discover. They are both bound to 31 years of age, and no doubt will endeavour to pass for free. *Samuel* lately brought a suit for his freedom in the General Court, which was determined against him. Whoever delivers the said servants to me, about two miles from *Michaux's* ferry, shall receive a reward of 6 l. if taken in *Virginia,* and if out of the colony 10 l.
WADE NETHERLAND.

free their own slaves. One of Jefferson's first actions in the House of Burgesses was to propose a law that would permit them to do so. He was shouted down, and his proposal was defeated.

Tom was convinced that slavery was a terrible sin. But his wealth and the success of his plantation was based upon the evil practice. In his heart, he knew slavery was wrong, and he constantly worked to end it by law—though he never freed his own slaves during his lifetime.

It did not take long for the other Burgesses to discover the new member's best talents. Thomas Jefferson was not an inspiring speaker, but it soon became apparent that he could write better than anyone else. His language was elegant, clear, and persuasive, and he was often called upon to write the drafts of committee resolutions, laws, and other papers.

CHAPTER FOUR

TRAGEDIES AND JOYS

"In every scheme of happiness she is placed in the foreground of the picture as the principal figure. Take that away, and it is no picture for me."
—Thomas Jefferson, writing about his wife, Martha

Jefferson was traveling for his law practice in February 1770 when he received shocking news. There had been a terrible fire at Shadwell. The place in which he had been born, the home shared with his mother and sisters, had burned almost to the ground. The servant who brought the news reported to Jefferson that the family was safe and his fiddle had been rescued, but all his books were destroyed. Jefferson had been collecting the books for years. Just like that, they were gone. "Would to God it had been money," he wrote to a friend. "Then it never would have cost me a sigh." For Jefferson, books were more precious than gold. In the next two years, he collected a new library of 1,250 books.

Work had begun on Monticello while Jefferson was living at Shadwell. While the damage to Shadwell was being repaired, he stepped up the construction work on his dream home on Little Mountain. Jefferson did not hire an architect to create the plans for his home. He studied buildings of the past and present and taught himself as much about architecture as any professional. He drew up his own plans for the house and gardens. He even sketched details for the other buildings that were needed on a southern plantation. These included kitchens and laundries, stables and dairies, and the smokehouse for preserving foods. It was the main house, however, that Jefferson

——————————— ✧ ———————————

Jefferson's vision for Monticello included many elements from classic Italian architecture, such as the columns in his first drawing of the home.

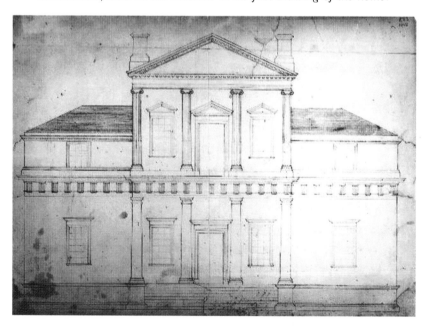

labored over most. He tinkered constantly with the design. He had a vision of a house and gardens different from any other in America. He wanted it to have timeless beauty, be graceful, and appeal to all the senses. At the same time, it had to be a comfortable home. Monticello was to be a reflection of Thomas Jefferson.

A visitor from France later commented, "No object had escaped Mr. Jefferson; and it seemed as if from his youth he had placed his mind, as he had done his house, on an elevated situation, from which he might contemplate the universe." Soon after the fire at Shadwell, a small brick out-building on Little Mountain was completed. It was a tiny space, but Jefferson was so eager to be living at Monticello that he moved in.

LOVE AND MARRIAGE

During this time, Thomas Jefferson met a twenty-one-year-old widow named Martha Wayles Skelton. Martha was the daughter of his friend and fellow attorney John Wayles. He described John Wayles as "a most agreeable companion, full of pleasantry and good humor." Martha had married young, but she had lost her husband soon after their marriage. When Jefferson met her, she had a three-year-old son. Jefferson adored the boy, but he died of a childhood illness before he turned four.

Martha was beautiful and accomplished. She was tall and slim "with a lithe and exquisitely formed figure, with a graceful and queenlike carriage." She was well educated and could discuss books and current events. She and Jefferson had much in common, most of all their interest in music. Just as he had with his sister

Jane, he accompanied Martha on the violin while she sang. Sometimes she played the harpsichord, and on other occasions, they sang together.

Martha was cheerful, charming, and popular. She had many suitors. One day, two of the suitors stood outside a room in Martha's home. They heard Martha and Jefferson deeply engrossed in their music. At that moment, his rivals realized that this shared love of music gave Tom Jefferson an advantage they could not overcome. They gave up their attempts to woo Martha.

Jefferson and Martha spent more and more time together. He often visited her at the Forest, her father's home, where she was living. Their love deepened with each month that passed. On January 1, 1772, surrounded by family and friends, Thomas Jefferson and Martha Wayles Skelton were married at the Forest. It was a happy occasion. The sound of fiddlers added to the merriment. Jefferson was twenty-nine, and Martha was twenty-three. They set off on the one-hundred-mile trip to begin their life together at Monticello.

On the way, they ran into a raging snowstorm. It was the worst in many years. Soon two feet of snow covered the narrow roads. They had to abandon the coach and continue on horseback. Swirling snow swept over them. A bitter wind pierced their clothing and tore at their faces. Cold and tired, they finally arrived at Monticello. Jefferson and his new wife had to make their way in the dark to the little brick outbuilding where they were to live while the main house was being completed. All the fires had gone out, and the servants were asleep in their own houses. The building contained one room, eighteen feet square. The small space, Jefferson wrote, served for "parlor, for kitchen and hall . . . for bedchamber and study, too." This could have been an unpleasant beginning to a marriage. Instead, the young couple treated it as a delightful adventure. They laughed and joked as they lit candles and set them about the small house. The room was filled with books and comfortable furniture. They had wine and music and each other. Later, Jefferson described to a friend how he and Martha "refreshed themselves . . . and startled the silence of the night with song and merry laughter." This profound understanding and love would mark all their days together.

──────────────── ✧ ────────────────

Jefferson and Martha spent their first winter together in this small cabin.

MONTICELLO

Our own dear Monticello ... mountains, forests, rocks, rivers. With what majesty do we ride above the storms.
   —Thomas Jefferson

Monticello (above), the house and estate of Thomas Jefferson, is located in Albemarle County, Virginia, near the city of Charlottesville. Jefferson's first design for Monticello called for fourteen rooms. As time passed, he continued to make changes and add details. It took thirty-nine years before the main building of forty-three rooms was completed in 1809.

Jefferson invented a ceiling compass for his home that is connected to a weather vane on the roof. This device indicates the strength and direction of the wind to those inside the house. A clock in the hall is operated by cannonball weights. It shows the day of the week as well as the time. Jefferson also designed a dumbwaiter to bring wine up from the cellar, and he eased food service between the kitchen and dining room by installing a revolving door. Monticello had five privies (bathrooms). Two were inside, which was unusual for the time.

The style of the main house at Monticello is called "neoclassic" because it is based on ancient Greek and Roman —or classical—designs. It is made of red brick trimmed with white wood and has a white dome on top. In front is a portico, or porch, with tall Greek columns.

Jefferson was more than $107,000 in debt when he died in 1826. His heir, his only surviving daughter Martha, was forced to sell the house and estate. The new owner neglected Monticello. Thomas Jefferson's beautiful estate might have become a ruin if it had not been for Uriah P. Levy, a naval officer. Levy was a great admirer of Jefferson. He visited Monticello in 1834 and was sad to see the terrible condition of the president's beloved home. Levy purchased Monticello and repaired it. He believed it should be a national monument and planned to donate it to the American people. Before that could happen, the Civil War (1861–1865) broke out and Southern forces seized Monticello. It was not returned to the Levy family until 1879. Levy's nephew and his heirs spent millions of dollars to preserve the estate. In 1923 they sold it to the Thomas Jefferson Foundation. Both the house and plantation have been completely restored and are open to the public.

Not long after the marriage, Martha's father died. Martha's inheritance almost doubled the size of the Jeffersons' property. Many slaves were included. Jefferson, an opponent of slavery, owned even more slaves than before.

On September 27, 1772, Martha gave birth to their first child, a daughter, also named Martha but called Patsy. Patsy was sickly at first, and for months her parents worried whether she would survive. Many children in those days died during infancy, but Patsy grew strong and healthy.

Thomas Jefferson's life was busier than ever. He had to supervise the running of thousands of acres of farmland as well as the construction of Monticello. His law practice brought him as many cases as he could handle. He and Martha enjoyed their time together and with friends. They often saw Dabney Carr and his family. Carr was also a successful lawyer. Like Jefferson, he was a member of the House of Burgesses. Unlike Jefferson, he was an exciting speaker. After his first speech, people predicted that he would have a brilliant future. Jefferson was thrilled by his friend's triumph. "I will remember," he wrote, "the pleasure expressed in the . . . conversation of the members . . . on the debut of Mr. Carr, and the hopes they conceived as well from his talents as its patriotism."

Soon after that promising speech, Dabney Carr fell ill. An infection quickly spread through his body, and on May 16, 1773, he died. Jefferson was away at the time. As soon as he heard the terrible news, he hurried home to discover that his friend had already been buried at Shadwell. Jefferson had not forgotten the pledge he and Dabney Carr had made so many years before. He moved his friend's body to a spot near the old oak tree on Little Mountain where they had spent so many hours sharing their most intimate thoughts. On Dabney Carr's gravestone, Jefferson had inscribed, "To his Virtue, Good Sense, Learning, and Friendship this stone is dedicated by Thomas Jefferson, who of all men living, loved him most."

Carr's widow, Martha, Jefferson's sister, had loved her husband deeply. His early death devastated her and their six young children. Jefferson assured his sister that he would always take care of her and the children and soon moved them all into his own home. His second daughter, Jane Randolph, came into the world on April 3, 1774.

Jefferson's private life and domestic cares seemed over-whelming. Outside events were occurring, however, that would sweep Jefferson into a world of ideas and action.

CHAPTER FIVE

SEEDS OF REVOLUTION

"The God who gave us life
gave us liberty at the same time."
—Thomas Jefferson

During most of the 1700s, the thirteen American colonies belonged to Great Britain. Americans thought of themselves as British citizens. They were loyal subjects of the king and proud to be part of the most powerful empire on earth.

Gradually, differences appeared between the settlers and their mother country. A spirit of independence emerged as generations born in the colonies grew to adulthood. Pioneers tamed the wilderness and overcame hardships to build farms and cities. They began to see themselves as Virginians, Pennsylvanians, or even as Americans.

In 1765, when Thomas Jefferson was nearing the completion of his law studies, the British Parliament had passed the Stamp Act. British soldiers, with help from colonials, had recently fought the French and Indian War on

American soil. Parliament and the king decided that the Americans should help pay for that war. The Stamp Act decreed that colonists had to pay a tax on every document they used, including bills of sale, wills, deeds, diplomas, and even newspapers.

The new tax was hard to bear. Even worse to the colonists was the fact that they had no say about it. Voters in Great Britain elected members to Parliament, but the colonists had no vote. They called the new law "taxation without

─────────────── ✧ ───────────────

This table shows the tax payable on different types of paper and printed goods as a result of the Stamp Act of 1765.

STAMP-OFFICE,
Lincoln's-Inn, 1765.

A

T A B L E

Of the Prices of Parchment and Paper for the Service
of *America.*

Parchment.   Paper.

Skins 18 Inch. by 13, at Fourpence   Horn at Seven-pence
22 ── by 16, at Six-pence   Fools Cap at Nine-pence
26 ── by 20, at Eight-pence } each.   D° with printed Notices } at
28 ── by 23, at Ten-pence   for Indentures   } 1 s. } each Quire,
31 ── by 26, at Thirteen-pence   Folio Post at One Shilling
                                        Demy ── at Two Shillings
                                        Medium at Three Shillings
                                        Royal ── at Four Shillings
                                        Super Royal at Six Shillings

Paper for Printing

News,   Almanacks.

Double Crown at 14 s. } each Ream.   Book──Crown Paper at 10 s. 6 d.
Double Demy at 19 s.   Book──Fools Cap at 6 s. 6 d. } each Ream.
                                        Pocket ── Folio Post at 20 s.
                                        Sheet──Demy at 13 s.

King George III enforced
many harsh policies against
the American colonists.
✧ ——————————

representation." Petitions were sent to the British Parliament and to King George III asking them to repeal the tax. The pleas were ignored, and resentment grew throughout the colonies. In Virginia a debate took place in the House of Burgesses. Thomas Jefferson's friend, Patrick Henry, made a passionate speech saying that only elected representatives of the people had the right to impose laws. He ended his argument by declaring, "Caesar had his Brutus [In ancient Rome, Brutus assassinated Julius Caesar], Charles the First his Cromwell [Oliver Cromwell executed this king of England in 1649], and George the Third. . . . "

At this point, Patrick Henry was interrupted by shouts of "Treason! Treason!" He continued, "And George the Third may profit by their example. If this be treason, make the most of it."

The young law student, Thomas Jefferson, had watched the proceedings from the doorway. Jefferson wrote that he had "heard the splendid display of Mr. Henry's talents as a popular orator—great indeed."

Patrick Henry's speech inspired a storm of outrage. People rioted and refused to pay the hated tax. In Boston anti-British feeling was so strong that citizens formed an organization called the Sons of Liberty. Soon there were Sons of Liberty in every colony. Two years later, Parliament repealed the Stamp Act.

The colonists were jubilant, but King George and Parliament were angry with their restless subjects. They found a new way to raise money in 1767. The Townshend Act required the colonists to pay a tax on almost every item imported from Great Britain. This tax caused even more hardship than the Stamp Act, since most of the goods used in the colonies came from England and other parts of the British Empire. The colonists were enraged. Violent protests erupted.

The British royal governor, Baron de Botecourt, punished the colonist by dissolving, or shutting down, the House of Burgesses. Twenty-eight burgesses continued to meet at the Raleigh Tavern in Williamsburg. Thomas Jefferson was among them. So were George Washington and Patrick Henry. They agreed to stop buying goods from British merchants. They would have to do without new clothing, spices, tea, paint, and jewelry. Committees were formed all over Virginia to support this

──────────── ✧
The colonists rioted in fierce protest of the taxes imposed by the British.

boycott. Jefferson worked hard to organize citizens in his own county of Albemarle. Late that year, Governor de Botecourt called for new elections for the House of Burgesses. Almost all the old members were reelected.

British merchants were hurt by these boycotts. They persuaded Parliament to cancel the taxes. The only one left in place was a tax on tea. By this time, the idea of freedom from British rule was spreading among the colonists. Thomas Jefferson was among them. Everything he had learned during his years of study convinced him that King George's actions were unjust and illegal. This kind of oppression, he declared, "plainly prove a . . . systematic plan for reducing us to slavery."

PROTESTS GROW IN THE COLONIES

In 1773 in Boston, a group of Patriots (people who believed the American colonies should be free) protested the tax on tea. Dressed as Native Americans, they boarded a ship in Boston Harbor and tossed the tea overboard. This "Boston Tea Party" infuriated King George. The British closed Boston Harbor and sent troops of red-coated British soldiers to control the colony. Virginia supported the Boston Patriots with a period of fasting and prayer. Angrily, Lord Dunmore, the new governor of Virginia, closed down the House of Burgesses again.

The Virginia representatives ignored the governor's command and continued to meet. In 1774 Thomas Jefferson summed up their thoughts in a series of resolutions called *A Summary View of the Rights of British America.* He argued that the colonists' ancestors were free people in England before they came to the colonies. They were still free people,

Tired of being oppressed by British taxes, Patriots decided to protest. They boarded a ship loaded with tea and threw the entire shipment into the harbor.

──────── ✧ ────────

but they had no representatives in the British Parliament. Without colonists' representation, he declared, Parliament "has no right to exercise its authority over us." He begged King George to cooperate with the colonists to achieve peace and harmony. The *Summary View* was published and read throughout the colonies. Jefferson's resolutions caught the public's imagination. The colonists had taken for granted their allegiance to the king. They began to question it. Jefferson suggested that people had the right to choose their own government.

These ideas might have faded if the British king and Parliament had been willing to listen to the colonists' demands. Instead, they sent in more British troops, enforced curfews, and arrested protesters. This only brought more resistance. In the fall of 1774, a Continental Congress was called to meet in Philadelphia. Representatives came from all the colonies but Georgia. Jefferson was unable to attend due to illness, but his fellow Virginian, Patrick Henry, was there. The delegates decided that the colonies must stand together against the tyranny of Great Britain. After the Congress finished its work, Virginia leaders met in Richmond to support its actions. Thomas Jefferson was present at this meeting. So was Patrick Henry, who declared, "Is life so dear or peace so sweet as to be purchased at the price of chains and slavery? . . . Give me liberty," he thundered, "or give me death!"

In April 1775, farmers in Massachusetts formed militias to protect themselves from the British soldiers that had been stationed there. Bloody battles were fought at Lexington and Concord between the militias and the British soldiers.

The American Revolution had begun.

————————— ✧
Patrick Henry (far right)
gave many impassioned speeches.

CHAPTER SIX

THE WAR YEARS

"When in the course of human events,
it becomes necessary for one people to dissolve
the political bands which have connected them
with another . . . they should declare the causes
which impel them to the separation."
—The Declaration of Independence

Thomas Jefferson was elected as a delegate from Virginia to the Second Continental Congress in Philadelphia. It met in the summer of 1775. Battles were raging between American militias and British troops, especially in and around Boston. King George and his generals were determined to put the colonists in their place. Some delegates still hoped they could come to an agreement with Great Britain. They drafted a letter of reconciliation to be sent to the king. He refused to read it. Most members of the Congress realized that the British government would never grant them representation and the freedom to govern themselves. A way had to be

The members of the Second Continental Congress debated for many long hours in Carpenters' Hall.

✧ ——————————

found to unite the colonies and even prepare for war. They debated all through that hot, sticky summer in Carpenters' Hall (later called Independence Hall).

Thomas Jefferson seldom spoke during debates on the floor. He was more comfortable expressing his opinions in small committees or with individuals. His writing skills were soon recognized though, and he was asked to draft committee reports and memos. Most of his ideas agreed with those of another delegate, John Adams from Massachusetts. Like Jefferson, Adams was a brilliant scholar and writer. He, too, was a champion of liberty and believed that separation from Great Britain was the only possible course. Thomas Jefferson and John Adams were opposites in many ways. One was a southern gentleman, the other a northern farmer. Jefferson was tall and lean, and Adams was short and stout. Adams was outgoing and talkative. Jefferson was reserved and quiet. Despite these differences, they became good friends. They shared a passion for learning and knowledge. They both believed in the Patriot cause and recognized that what happened in Philadelphia would affect the course of history. Adams wrote admiringly about his new friend, "He was so prompt, frank . . . and decisive upon committees and in conversation . . . that he soon seized my heart."

Jefferson also met Benjamin Franklin of Pennsylvania, the elder statesman of the Congress. Franklin had gray hair and a wrinkled face. But his eyes sparkled with wit and wisdom. Franklin was admired abroad as well as at home. He was famous as a printer, inventor, writer, and scientist.

Soon after Jefferson's arrival in Philadelphia, his fellow Virginian George Washington was appointed commander in chief of the Continental Army. He organized the various town militias into one fighting force. The British were bringing in seasoned troops to crush the colonists. The Americans were determined to resist British oppression, but

———————————————— ◇ ————————————————

Jefferson maintained close friendships with both Benjamin Franklin (left) and John Adams (right).

they were untrained for battle. General Washington's task was to organize these volunteers, who were mostly farmers, into an effective fighting force. Hopes were high. A new ballad compared Washington to the most famous general of ancient times, Alexander the Great:

> We have a bold commander, who fears not sword
>   nor gun
> The second Alexander—his name is Washington.

FAMILY CONCERNS

Although Jefferson worked tirelessly as debates continued into the fall, his heart was at Monticello. He worried about crops and harvesting. His thoughts were always wandering back to his two little daughters and his wife, Martha, who was often ill. In September 1775, he rode home for a short visit to find that another tragedy had struck the family. His eighteen-month-old baby, Jane Randolph Jefferson, had sickened and died. Martha's grief made her poor health even worse. Jefferson hated leaving her at such a time, but duty called him to Philadelphia.

Jefferson's work for the Congress was important, but it became harder and harder for him to bear the separation from his family. He wrote letters home regularly but heard nothing in return for almost two months. "The suspense under which I am is too terrible to be endured," he wrote in a letter to his brother-in-law. "If anything has happened, for god's sake, let me know it."

Finally, Jefferson received a letter from Martha saying that all was well. Nevertheless, he feared for the health and safety of his family. Virginia, like the other colonies, was torn by fighting. Lord Dunmore, the governor, proclaimed martial law. This meant that the British military ruled the citizens of Virginia. British soldiers burned down the city of Norfolk on the Atlantic Coast. Dunmore also widened the divisions among Virginians by rewarding those who would defend King George's rule. The governor even offered to free slaves who joined his army. Jefferson could stay away no longer. In December, although Congress was still meeting, he set off for Monticello.

Jefferson remained at Monticello for four months. Martha needed him. She was frail and heartbroken over the loss of their child. Jefferson also had to care for his mother, who was gravely ill. On March 31, 1776, he wrote in his diary, "My mother died about eight o'clock this morning, in the 57th year of her age." Jefferson mourned the loss of his mother. For many weeks, he suffered terrible headaches that lasted entire days. He described them as "paroxysms [sudden attacks] of the most excruciating pain."

In spite of these personal problems, Jefferson continued to work for the American cause. He was elected to the Committee of Safety in Albemarle County, which directed the colonial militia there. He collected a supply of gunpowder for the Virginia militia and raised money to be sent to Boston. Its harbor was blockaded (closed) by British ships, and food and other supplies were dwindling. He worked closely with other Patriots in Virginia to draft a resolution declaring Virginia a free and independent state.

Early in 1776, Jefferson read a pamphlet that thrilled him. It was called *Common Sense* and was written by Thomas Paine, a recent immigrant from England. Paine called upon Americans to create a democratic nation.

Common Sense inspired the Patriots and fired their determination. But Thomas Jefferson was getting ready to write a document that would eclipse even Paine's ringing words.

DECLARATION OF INDEPENDENCE

Jefferson returned to Philadelphia in May 1776. He was appointed to a committee that would write an official explanation of why the colonies were separating from Great Britain and seal the Patriots' commitment to independence. Others on the committee included Franklin and Adams. They agreed that Thomas Jefferson should draft this important declaration. "You can write ten times better than I can," Adams told him.

Jefferson retired to rooms he had rented on the second floor of a house owned by a bricklayer named Graaf. He dipped his quill pen into the inkpot and began to write. The reading and thinking he had crammed into his thirty-three years of life came together to produce a Declaration of Independence that brought a new era to the world. "We hold these truths to be self-evident," he wrote, "that all men are created equal, that they are endowed by their Creator with certain unalienable Rights, that among these are Life, Liberty, and the pursuit of Happiness."

The delegates signed the Declaration on July 4, 1776. It was a solemn moment. Each man knew that if the Patriot cause failed, they would lose all they possessed and probably be hanged for treason. With their signatures, they pledged to each other, "our Lives, our Fortunes, and our sacred Honor."

Jefferson's first draft of the Declaration had included a call for an end to the slave trade. To his regret, this was eliminated from the final version. The most important task at this crucial hour was to unite the colonies.

*In this famous painting by John Trumbull, the delegates
gather to sign the Declaration of Independence. Jefferson
is standing at the front of the group at the table.*

———————————— ◇ ————————————

Representatives from the southern states would never sign a
document that abolished the slave trade.

Copies of the Declaration were carried by horseback
and wagon to every corner of the colonies. In large cities
and small villages, citizens gathered to hear it read. Bells
rang out and people cheered. A new nation was born.

Even before the signing of the Declaration of Independence, the struggle for freedom was not going well.
Fourteen thousand citizens had fled when the British occupied Boston. George Washington had rushed the
Continental Army to nearby Cambridge, Massachusetts,
where he received a hero's welcome. John Adams's wife,
Abigail, described him as having "dignity with ease." But

Washington did not have time for social events. He had only an army of untrained volunteers to prevent British forces from advancing into the countryside. When the British left Boston and headed to New York, Washington had to quickly march his troops south to meet the expected attack.

Superior British forces, commanded by General William Howe, defeated the Continental soldiers in New York City and Long Island, New York. Washington's army suffered terrible losses and was forced to retreat. The British pursued the shattered Continental forces across New Jersey. In December 1776, those who were left rowed across the Delaware River to Pennsylvania. Things looked bleak for the Americans.

Their hopes rose when George Washington took his troops back across the Delaware on Christmas Eve for a

———————————————— ✧ ————————————————

This famous painting by Emanuel Leutze depicts General Washington leading his troops across the Delaware River.

Many American soldiers did not survive the harsh winter at Valley Forge.

─────────────── ✧ ───────────────

surprise victory over Hessian troops, German soldiers who had been hired to fight for the British. But there were many more defeats than victories during the next few years. One of the lowest points for the colonists occurred during the winter of 1777–1778 when American soldiers froze, sickened, and died at their winter camp at Valley Forge, Pennsylvania.

Virginia was spared from the worst of the fighting for several years. During that period, Thomas Jefferson spent time with his family at the place he loved best—the green, golden hills of Monticello. "Peach trees and cherry trees at Monticello begin to blossom," he wrote in his notebook. He continued work on the house and studied astronomy and meteorology. In May 1777, Martha Jefferson gave birth to a son, but the baby died. A year later, though, the

Jeffersons rejoiced at the birth of a healthy daughter. They named her Mary, nicknamed Polly.

NEW GOVERNMENT FOR VIRGINIA

Jefferson served on committees of the House of Delegates, the new government that was being set up in Virginia. He believed that the colonies would achieve independence, and he wanted the new nation to establish a government that would represent and protect the people. He hoped to take the first steps in Virginia. Jefferson felt it was important for the citizens of a democracy to be educated and able to support themselves. He wanted a public school system that would provide every child in Virginia with a good education. He urged laws to establish small farms for people who had no land so they could be self-sufficient. He also offered a measure that would eventually end slavery. The older members of the legislature voted down all these proposals.

Jefferson had a deep belief in the freedom of religion and the separation of church and state. In Virginia, as in Great Britain and the other colonies, the Anglican Church (or Church of England) was supported by the government. It was the official church of all the people, and they all had to pay taxes to support it. Jefferson wrote an Ordinance for Religious Freedom stating that "all men shall be free to profess and maintain . . . their opinions in matter of religion." The Virginia legislature finally adopted Jefferson's freedom of religion laws, and he believed it was one of his most important achievements.

CHAPTER SEVEN

WAR COMES TO VIRGINIA

*"History will never relate the horrors
committed by the British army
in the Southern States of America."*
—Thomas Jefferson

In 1779 Thomas Jefferson's fellow Virginians elected him governor. He was thirty-six years old. The new governor of Virginia had high hopes and many plans. He wanted Virginia to be a model for the new country. But Thomas Jefferson took office just when the state came under attack from the British. All his energies were consumed with the war and the dangers facing the people of Virginia.

A month before Jefferson took office, a British fleet attacked Virginia. Eighteen thousand British redcoats marched through the countryside. They destroyed crops and supplies and burned whole towns to the ground. Governor Jefferson worked tirelessly at the new state capital in Richmond, where the government had moved for safety in the spring of 1780.

Benedict Arnold was an American military hero who turned traitor to fight for the British.

✧ ————————

He tried desperately to obtain troops and supplies, but the state was almost bankrupt. What few resources Virginians possessed had to be shared with the main Continental forces that were fighting and starving with General Washington. The Virginia militia was poorly trained. It lacked arms and supplies and could not stop the onslaught.

In January 1781, the British, led by Benedict Arnold, took Richmond. Arnold had fought on the American side earlier in the struggle, but he had turned traitor and was leading a British army. The British troops under General Arnold set fire to Richmond. The state government had to flee to Charlottesville, not far from Jefferson's home.

Governor Jefferson wrote desperate letters to Congress, but no help came. Personal problems added to Jefferson's despair. In April 1780, Martha had given birth to their fifth child. The infant died in 1781, and Martha's health worsened. By June the British were advancing toward Charlottesville.

Jefferson rushed to Monticello. He hurried his family into a carriage and sent them off to safety at another plantation. He stayed behind and, leaving his horse at a crossroads, set off up nearby Carter's Mountain with a telescope. From there he had a perfect view of Charlottesville. The streets appeared to be quiet and empty. Jefferson breathed a sigh of relief. He decided there was no danger and began to walk back toward home. He turned to glance once more through the telescope. In the few minutes he had looked away, the streets of Charlottesville had filled with red-coated soldiers. Monticello was at their mercy. The governor ran to his horse and galloped off just in time. Ten minutes later, British troops swarmed over Jefferson's home.

The house was empty except for two slaves, who had just hidden the family silver in a secret place under the floor. The British demanded to know where Jefferson was. A soldier pointed a pistol at Martin, one of the slaves, and threatened to shoot if he did not reveal Jefferson's whereabouts. The slaves of Monticello were loyal to Thomas

The British often set fire to farms and towns as they marched through.

Jefferson, who had treated them kindly. "Fire away!" Martin told the soldier bravely. The redcoat put down his pistol.

The British commander, Lord Banastre Tarleton, commanded his troops to leave Monticello as they had found it, so no damage was done. Another British general acted quite differently. General Cornwallis's army captured a house at Elk Hill, another part of the Jefferson plantation. The British made it their headquarters. They stole anything they could use and destroyed everything else. They burned crops, fences, and barns, and slit the throats of young colts that were of no value to them. The slaves who lived at Elk Hill thought that the British would free them. Instead, the soldiers seized the slaves and forced them to remain in the British camp, where most died of smallpox or fever.

VICTORY FOR THE AMERICANS

The tide of the war began to turn. In 1780–1781, the French came to the aid of the colonists, and French ships blockaded the British along the Virginia coast. Thousands of French troops had landed to assist the American army. A combined force of American and French troops met the British army at Yorktown, Virginia. A fierce battle followed. This time, the redcoats were outmanned and outfought. British troops surrendered and laid down their arms on October 19, 1781, as a British band played "The World Turned Upside Down." Skirmishes continued for another year, but the American Revolution truly came to a victorious end at Yorktown.

Shortly before the battle of Yorktown, Jefferson decided to resign as governor. He was tired of politics and

This painting by John Trumbull depicts the surrender
of British troops at Yorktown in 1781.

——————————— ✧ ———————————

petty bickering. He felt he had given all he could to his
state and the new republic. Many Virginians blamed the
governor for their troubles. Some charged him with cow-
ardice for fleeing Charlottesville instead of staying to
fight. The Virginia legislature demanded the governor's
presence at a session to explain his actions. Jefferson
pointed out that escaping the city was a sign of prudence,
not a cowardly act. The legislators were ashamed and
embarrassed that they had questioned Jefferson's behavior.
They voted unanimously for a motion thanking Jefferson
for his services. But he was deeply hurt and vowed never
again to take part in politics.

Thomas Jefferson went home to Monticello." I have
retired to my farm, my family, and my books," he wrote to a
friend, "from which I think nothing will ever more separate

me." Soon after his return, he had an accident. He was thrown violently from his horse and was seriously injured. He could not leave the house for many weeks. But someone suggested a task that would keep him busy.

A NEW PROJECT

Jefferson received a letter from a French diplomat in Philadelphia named Francois de Barbe-Marbois. He wanted information about Virginia. He asked twenty-one questions on a variety of subjects. This was a perfect project for Thomas Jefferson. It was an adventure of the mind, to which he could bring his incredible knowledge of Virginia. He took up his pen and began to describe his state in all its aspects. He outlined the geography including rivers, cities, ports, boundaries, and mountains. He described the native forests, wildlife, trees, flowers, and fruit. The people and their ways of life were set forth in detail, including the problems and the evils of slavery. "I tremble for my country," he wrote, "when I reflect that God is just, that his justice cannot sleep forever." Native Americans, whose culture had always interested him, were also included. He wrote about their origins, histories, and languages. He discussed the political and social dreams he had for his state and for America, emphasizing public education and freedom of religion.

"Millions of innocent men, women and children, since the introduction of Christianity, have been burnt, tortured, fined, imprisoned," he wrote, "but it does me no injury for my neighbor to say there are twenty gods, or no god." His answers developed into essays, then into chapters, and finally into a book. A copy of *Notes on the State of Virginia* was sent to Barbe-Marbois on December

Jefferson wrote extensively about Virginia in his letters
to the French diplomat Francois de Barbe-Marbois.

20, 1781. A letter from the author claimed it was "very
imperfect and not worth offering."

Notes on the State of Virginia contained many private
thoughts, and Jefferson had no intention of publishing them.
He showed the volume only to a few close friends. They
begged him to publish it for the education of the public. He
refused, even when John Adams said, "The passages upon
slavery are worth diamonds." Four years later, Jefferson
finally permitted a small edition of two hundred copies to be
printed in France. Even then, he removed his name from the
title page. Eventually, the book was printed in Great Britain

and America. *Notes on the State of Virginia* is still read. It is not only a description of one state and one period in a nation's history, it is also a portrait of a great mind.

The months that followed Jefferson's recovery from the accident were among the happiest in his life. He worked on his book about Virginia. He filled logbooks with notes concerning crops and prices. His daughters, Patsy and Polly, received much attention and instruction from their father. He also looked after his widowed sister's six children, who lived at Monticello with their mother. And he continued to supervise the building of Monticello.

Best of all, he spent most of his time with Martha. They worked in harmony on the details of running a house and plantation. They shared their love of music and conversation with each other and a small group of good friends. Martha was not in good health, and she was also pregnant again. But she bravely carried out her duties amid expressions of love for her husband and children.

TRAGEDY STRIKES

In April 1782, their sixth child, Lucy, was born, leaving Martha ill and weak. Her condition continued to worsen. Jefferson was frantic. All his attention became focused on his wife. For months he insisted on caring for her himself. His daughter Patsy described her father during this time. "As a nurse, no female ever had more tenderness nor anxiety. He nursed my poor mother . . . sitting up with her and administering her medicines and drink to the last . . . he was never out of calling."

It was a hopeless struggle. On September 6, 1782, Martha Jefferson died. Jefferson's grief was unbearable.

"The violence of his emotion," his daughter wrote, "to this day I dare not describe to myself."

Jefferson shut himself up in his room and did not come out for three weeks. His family and friends worried for his safety and sanity. The Thomas Jefferson who finally emerged was a different man. His eyes were hollow, and his face was worn by sorrow. He tried to lose himself in mindless activity. "He was incessantly on horseback," Patsy wrote, "rambling about the mountains . . . roads and . . . through the woods." His correspondence lay on the desk unanswered for months. Finally, he wrote to a friend, "A single event wiped away all my plans and left me a blank, which I had not the spirit to fill in."

Thomas Jefferson had hoped to live out his life in peaceful retirement with Martha at Monticello. But that could never be. He had engraved on Martha's tombstone:

> *To the Memory of*
> MARTHA JEFFERSON
> *Daughter of John Wayles;*
> *Born October 19th, 1748*
> *Married* THOMAS JEFFERSON
> *January 1, 1772*
> *Torn from him by Death*
> *September 6th, 1782*
> *This Monument of his Love is inscribed*

Thomas Jefferson never married again.

CHAPTER EIGHT

BACK TO PUBLIC SERVICE

*"I was much an enemy of monarchy before I
came to Europe. I am ten thousand times more
so since I have seen what they are."*
—Thomas Jefferson

Thomas Jefferson was a widower with three small daughters—Patsy, ten; Polly, four; and the baby, Lucy. Months passed after Martha's death, but Jefferson's grief did not lessen. For the rest of his life, he carried a paper in his pocket on which he had written, "There is a time in human suffering when exceeding sorrows are but like snow falling on an iceberg." He spent time with his children and rode about the plantation, silent and brooding. Patsy became her father's constant companion. She followed him all over, sticking to him like a shadow, trying to ease his pain.

Jefferson's friends were concerned. Some of them decided that this might be a good time for him to return to public service. He was asked by Congress to be part of a team in Paris, France, that was working on a peace treaty with Great Britain. The fighting had ended, but an official treaty had not yet been signed. The other members of the American delegation, including Benjamin Franklin and John Adams, were already in Paris.

Thomas Jefferson had thought he would never leave Monticello again, but the main reason for him to stay there was gone. He accepted the offer and traveled to Philadelphia in November 1782 to board a ship for Europe. The ship was unable to sail because it was stuck in the thick ice. Jefferson stayed in Philadelphia for three months, waiting for the ice to melt. During that time, he renewed his interest in government and met with old friends.

Jefferson was still in Philadelphia when the discussions in Paris ended and a treaty was signed. There was no longer any reason for him to go to France. In 1783 he was elected as a delegate to Congress, where important decisions were being made.

He left Monticello in November to join the new government. While serving in Congress, Jefferson wrote frequently to his children. He constantly expressed his love and concern for them and instructed them on their education and behavior. Jefferson believed that women should be as well educated as men, and he encouraged his daughters in their learning. In one letter to Patsy, he suggested an effective way to use her time:

From 8 to 10, practice music.
From 10 to 1, dance one day and draw another.
From 1 to 2, draw on the day you dance, and write a letter next day.

From 3 to 4, read French.
From 4 to 5, exercise yourself in music.
From 5 till bedtime, read English, write, etc.

In 1783 America was not a unified country. It was a loose combination of thirteen states. The power of Congress was limited, and this caused all sorts of problems. It was essential to set up a central government and laws. Jefferson immediately began drawing up plans for the new nation. He presented his ideas in detailed, clearly written documents. He designed a new system of money using dollars, dimes, and pennies. One of his most important contributions was a plan for bringing new states into the United States. Jefferson's proposal provided that a new state could be added when it had as many citizens as the smallest of the original thirteen states. The territory mapped out by Jefferson later became the states of Ohio, Indiana, Illinois, Michigan, and Wisconsin.

Once again, Congress asked him to go to France. This time, he was to join John Adams and Benjamin Franklin. They were to work on trade agreements with France to help strengthen the struggling economy of the new nation.

JEFFERSON IN PARIS

On July 5, 1784, Jefferson set sail out of Boston Harbor on a small ship called the *Ceres*. He left his younger daughters, Polly and Lucy, in the care of their mother's sister, Elizabeth Eppes. Patsy accompanied him to Paris. Jefferson had spent many hours reading and studying about the cultures of Europe. He was going to Paris, the cultural center of the Western world at the time.

Benjamin Franklin and John Adams were there to greet him. They had already begun discussions to obtain agreements that would permit the United States to trade freely with other nations. The Marquis de Lafayette, a French nobleman, also welcomed Jefferson to his country. They had become friends when Lafayette was in America fighting for the Patriot cause. Lafayette made sure that every door in Paris was open to Jefferson. He was able to socialize with the most interesting and talented people in France. He enjoyed the company of Franklin, with whom he shared

──────── ✧ ────────

*The Marquis de Lafayette (below) ensured
that Jefferson felt welcome in Paris.*

many interests. Jefferson also renewed his friendship with
John Adams and John's wife, Abigail. Abigail called
Jefferson "one of the choice ones of the world."

Paris was a feast of the mind for Jefferson. He walked
through the centuries-old streets, admiring the magnificent
buildings, gardens, and art galleries. He jotted down details
of architecture in his notebook. He purchased hundreds of
books at the stalls on the banks of the Seine River.

Jefferson also noted the horrors of eighteenth-century
Paris. A few aristocrats lived in splendor while masses of
men, women, and children knew only tyranny, poverty, and
hunger. He sympathized with the ideals of freedom and
equality that were springing up throughout France.
Jefferson's own writings were widely read and admired there.

Benjamin Franklin had represented U.S. interests in
France for many years. He was seventy-nine years old and
in poor health. In 1785 he decided to return home.
Congress appointed Thomas Jefferson the new minister to
France. Jefferson realized that it would be a long time
before he would be able to leave France. He wanted his
family together. He had Patsy, but Polly was still in Virginia
with her aunt. Little Lucy had died the year before at the
age of two. Lucy's death made Jefferson determined to have
his family together in Paris. But Polly refused to come. She
liked her life and friends in Virginia and wanted to stay
there. Her father had to trick her into joining him. She and
some friends were sent to play aboard a ship in the harbor.
They enjoyed themselves and went back time after time.
One day, after a morning of fun, the children took naps on
the ship. The other girls were quietly awakened and taken
away, and the ship set sail with the sleeping Polly aboard.

Jefferson greatly admired Parisian architecture,
such as this fountain in the Chatelet Square.

Polly was furious at first, but she soon began to enjoy the exciting journey. In Paris she was reunited with her father and sister, whom she hadn't seen in four years. They showered her with love and attention. She went to the same school as her sister, who watched over her. Polly soon began to enjoy life in Paris. She even called herself Maria, a French form of Mary, her real name, from then on.

Thomas Jefferson stayed abroad for five years. He negotiated trade agreements with the French that helped the United States pay off some of its debt from the war. He traveled to other European countries, expanding his

Jefferson's polygraph sits in his den in Monticello. A polygraph uses two pens attached to springs. What is written with one pen is automatically duplicated by the other.

———————— ✧ ————————

knowledge and understanding. He sketched or sent home examples of many ideas and objects new to him. Among these were a solar microscope, a thermometer, new types of rice, and methods to improve crops. His favorite purchase was a copy machine called a Watt press. Later, Jefferson invented his own copying device called a polygraph. He used this machine from then on, making a copy of every letter he wrote.

Jefferson was often invited to the French king's court and to gatherings of the nobility. He learned to move easily among all sorts of people—aristocrats and revolutionaries alike. He formed new friendships, including a close one with Maria Cosway. She was one of the most beautiful, talented, and popular women in Paris. She and Jefferson spent hours together sharing their interest in music, art, and literature.

While Jefferson carried out his duties in France, a Constitutional Convention was meeting in Philadelphia to write the basic laws for the new United States. Jefferson's fellow Virginian James Madison wrote to him almost daily, describing the discussions. Jefferson responded with frequent letters to Madison, Washington, and other friends, outlining his own thoughts. Many of his ideas were incorporated into the U.S. Constitution. Jefferson approved of most of the parts of the Constitution, but he was not satisfied until a Bill of Rights was added. Jefferson insisted this must include "freedom of religion, freedom of the press, protection against standing armies, . . . and trial by jury."

Meanwhile, conditions in France continued to worsen. Jefferson hoped that the king and queen would put reforms into effect, but they turned their backs on the suffering of their people. The winter of 1788–1789 was one of the coldest ever recorded in Paris. People froze and starved on street corners. The movement toward revolution grew stronger. Jefferson's friend Lafayette drew up a Declaration of the Rights of Man. It was

──────── ✦

James Madison (right) and Jefferson shared many ideas. Madison was instrumental in adding the Bill of Rights to the Constitution.

Angry Parisians force their way into the Bastille in 1789.

———————————— ✧ ————————————

inspired by the Declaration Jefferson himself had written in 1776. The king ignored all pleas for help. In July the desperate people of Paris stormed the Bastille jail and released all prisoners. The French Revolution had begun.

On September 16, 1789, Thomas Jefferson's request to return home was approved, and his long economic mission to Paris ended. Accompanied by Patsy and Maria (Polly), he boarded a ship at LeHavre, France, for the voyage home.

CHAPTER NINE

SECRETARY OF STATE
AND VICE PRESIDENT

"No government can continue good,
but under the control of the people."
—Thomas Jefferson

Thomas Jefferson and his children sailed back to America on the *Clermont*. Near the coast of the United States, they ran into rough weather. The ship was battered by a storm and caught fire. It was a frightening journey. The vessel finally reached Norfolk, and the passengers were able to leave the ship.

Jefferson had a lot of work to do at Monticello. The plantation had not been managed well during his absence, and he was in debt. He needed time to recover from financial problems. Then he hoped to return to France, which he thought of as his second home. But his nation called him to service again.

In April 1789, George Washington had taken the oath of office as the first president of the United States. Jefferson had written to him from Paris with congratulations. "There was nobody so well qualified as yourself," he wrote, "to put our new machine into a regular course of action."

Jefferson was home only a short time when he received the news that Washington had selected him to be secretary of state, one of a group of advisers to the president known as the cabinet. It would be his duty to oversee relations with foreign nations. Jefferson longed to stay at Monticello with his family. If he left, his financial problems would get worse. But the new nation was at a crossroads. Not many people believed that this experiment in democracy, government by the people, would last. The first administration would be particularly important. How it conducted the affairs of state would have an enormous effect on whether the nation would succeed or fail. Jefferson accepted the post. He would have to live in New York City, which was then the capital of the new country.

A happy family event kept him at Monticello a while longer. Seventeen-year-old Patsy had fallen in love with her third cousin, Thomas Mann Randolph Jr. They wanted to marry. Jefferson thought highly of Thomas Randolph. He was the son of Jefferson's cousin and close friend, Thomas Randolph Sr. "The marriage of your son with my daughter," he wrote to the bridegroom's father, "cannot be more pleasing to you than to me." Patsy and Thomas Randolph were married at Monticello on February 23, 1790. One week later, Thomas Jefferson left for his new position in New York.

Jefferson did not enjoy working in an office. He developed painful migraine headaches as he set to work on his new duties. He wrote a detailed report on weights and measures while suffering "severe headache which came on every day at sunrise and never left me till sunset."

Jefferson knew the other cabinet members and expected to work well with them. Trouble soon erupted, however, with Alexander Hamilton, the secretary of the treasury. Jefferson had faith in small farmers and ordinary people and opposed granting too much power to the central government. "Aristocrats fear the people," he warned, "and wish to transfer all power to the higher classes of society." Alexander Hamilton mistrusted rule by the people. He called the public a "great beast." He favored a strong central government with power in the hands of business owners and the wealthy.

Both Jefferson and Hamilton were brilliant and well informed. Each believed his philosophy of government was

best for the country. Their first clash came when Hamilton wanted the federal government to pay the debts the states had from fighting the revolution. Jefferson believed this would give too much power to the central government to interfere in the affairs of the states. Most southerners agreed with

✧ ————————

Alexander Hamilton (left), *secretary of the treasury, and Jefferson did not agree on how the new national government should operate.*

Jefferson. The southern states had already paid a large part of their own debts. They did not want to be taxed for the benefit of the North. In a compromise, Hamilton agreed to locate the permanent capital of the United States in the South. This eventually became Washington, D.C. In return, the southerners approved Hamilton's debt proposal.

Not all the differences between these strong-minded leaders were settled peacefully. Hamilton urged the creation of a national bank to control the money supply as part of a centralized financial system. Jefferson opposed this. He felt a large central bank would ignore the needs of individuals and small farmers. Jefferson knew that the Constitution stated that powers not specifically given to the federal government were reserved to the states. A national bank was not mentioned in the Constitution, so Jefferson argued that it would be unconstitutional. Hamilton pointed out that the Constitution gave Congress the power to make all laws that were necessary and proper. Jefferson lost this dispute when the Bank of the United States was created in 1791.

One of the main duties of the secretary of state is to advise the president on foreign policy. Here, too, Jefferson ran into difficulties with Alexander Hamilton.

Great Britain had refused to sign a trade agreement with the United States. Great Britain also violated the peace treaty that ended the American Revolution by holding onto British forts in the Northwest Territory, the name given at that time to land around the Great Lakes. Jefferson wanted to take a strong stand against the British by limiting trade with them, but Hamilton blocked his efforts.

Great Britain and France went to war in 1793. Jefferson and Hamilton had different opinions about this too. Jefferson had supported the French Revolution and continued to hope for the success of its new government. He wanted France to win its struggle against Great Britain. Hamilton was strongly pro-British and viewed with alarm the uprising of the French people. George Washington finally persuaded his cabinet to agree that the United States should remain neutral and not support either side.

RISE OF POLITICAL PARTIES

The differences between Hamilton and Jefferson led to the formation of political parties. Those who opposed Hamilton called themselves Republicans. (This later became the Democratic Party.) The Republicans looked to Thomas Jefferson as their leader. Hamilton and his supporters were called Federalists. This development saddened President Washington. He had stressed unity among his countrymen and feared that political parties could tear the nation apart.

Jefferson and John Adams, Washington's vice president, had been close friends since their time together in Paris. Adams was a Federalist, however, and politics began to drive them apart. They disagreed on how the government should be run. Adams published a volume called *Discourses on Davila*, which included criticisms of the French Revolution. Jefferson was devoted to the ideals of the French Revolution. He wrote a preface to a new book in which he called Adams's ideas political heresies (departure from a popular belief). Jefferson later claimed that the printer had included this sentence in error, but the damage had been done. Adams was insulted. Their relationship cooled.

The friction between the Federalists and Republicans grew ugly. At one point, Hamilton printed anonymous newspaper articles about Jefferson saying he should be removed from office. Later, Jefferson's supporters accused Hamilton of financial misdeeds.

Jefferson hated the political bickering. Late in 1793, he wrote a letter to the president, resigning his position as secretary of state. Washington begged him to stay, but Jefferson could no longer stand the ugliness of politics. He returned to Monticello in January 1794. He longed for "happiness in the lap and love of my family, in the society of my neighbors and my books . . . interest or affection in every bud that opens, in every breath that blows around me."

POLITICAL DEVELOPMENTS

Thomas Jefferson was safe and happy at Monticello, but he carefully watched political developments in his country. Two events in 1794 disturbed him. Farmers in western Pennsylvania were having a difficult time. They were deeply in debt, and a tax on whiskey seemed to be the last straw. They protested the tax, and some of them took up arms in the "Whiskey Rebellion." President Washington, following the advice of Alexander Hamilton, sent an army into Pennsylvania to crush the protesters. Jefferson was angry. He didn't think that U.S. troops should be used against poor Americans.

The other incident involved a new treaty with the British, who still occupied forts in the United States. British ships were also harassing U.S. ships and sailors on the high seas. President Washington sent John Jay to Great Britain to negotiate a treaty. Jefferson was disturbed

Farmers in Pennsylvania protested the tax on whiskey.

when he heard that the Jay Treaty gave in to the British on every point.

Still, Thomas Jefferson believed he would enjoy his beloved home for the rest of his life. In 1795 he brought Patsy's children to live with him at Monticello, leaving Patsy free to take care of her husband, who had become ill. He loved being surrounded by his family and breathing the pure air of Monticello. He felt his energy renewed. Much of each day was spent on horseback, riding through his plantations. He figured out new, efficient methods to plant and gather crops. He kept detailed lists in his journals. He tinkered with new inventions, such as a folding stool and an inflatable life preserver. He built the first swivel chair. In October 1797, Maria (Polly) Jefferson married her cousin Jack Eppes in a quiet ceremony at Monticello.

In 1796 George Washington had announced that he would not serve a third term. The Federalists nominated

John Adams for president. Jefferson's friend James Madison persuaded him to let the Republicans put Jefferson's name forward as a candidate. Adams won the election and became the second president of the United States. Jefferson came in second. According to the law at that time, this made him vice president.

VICE PRESIDENT UNDER JOHN ADAMS

On March 4, 1797, Thomas Jefferson, who was fifty-three years old, traveled again to Philadelphia, which had become the nation's capital. As vice president, his only responsibility was to preside over the Senate. He observed the confusion on the floor of the Senate and immediately wrote a book of rules, *A Manual of Parliamentary Procedure*, which is still in use.

President Adams was facing problems with the French. Along with everyone else, Jefferson watched in horror as the revolution in France turned into a massacre. He believed in the ideals of the French Revolution and still hoped that these ideals would not be lost in the bloodshed. The Federalists, however, were afraid that French influence

A MANUAL

OF

PARLIAMENTARY PRACTICE.

FOR THE USE

OF THE

SENATE OF THE UNITED STATES.

BY THOMAS JEFFERSON.

WASHINGTON CITY.

PRINTED BY SAMUEL HARRISON SMITH.

MDCCCI.

✧ ————————————
To help Senate sessions run smoothly, Jefferson penned this book of regulations.

could cause unrest in the United States. They passed a set of laws called the Alien and Sedition Acts. These laws gave the president power to expel from the country anyone he thought might be dangerous. The sedition act imposed fines and jail terms on writers and newspaper editors who made statements against the government. Jefferson felt that these laws violated freedom of speech. As vice president, however, he could not speak out against decisions of Adams's administration.

In December 1799, George Washington died at his home in Mount Vernon, Virginia. His last years had been saddened by the growing disunity in his country. The whole nation mourned the passing of the one man who was able to bring the opposing sides together.

Many people felt that Thomas Jefferson was the only person who could fill Washington's shoes. In 1800 the Republicans again nominated Jefferson to run for president against John Adams. A nasty campaign followed. Jefferson spent this time quietly at Monticello. He tried to ignore the articles and cartoons that showed him as a madman and a devilish atheist (someone who does not believe in God). When the votes were finally counted, Adams and the Federalists had been defeated. Thomas Jefferson would be the third president of the United States.

As third president of the United States, Jefferson stressed unity among all people and equal rights for every citizen.

CHAPTER TEN

PRESIDENT JEFFERSON

"We are all republicans.
We are all federalists."
—Thomas Jefferson, First Inaugural Address, 1801

On March 4, 1801, Thomas Jefferson took the oath of office as third president of the United States. Aaron Burr, a Republican from New York, was sworn in as vice president.

Jefferson was the first president to take office in Washington, D.C. The new capital city, which he had helped design, was still under construction. Only a few buildings were completed, rising out of acres of mud. Jefferson walked from his boardinghouse to the unfinished Capitol building. The new president dressed simply, in keeping with his belief that government must represent all the people. The *Alexandria Times* noted that "his dress was, as usual, that of a plain citizen without any distinctive badge of office."

In his inaugural speech, Jefferson reminded his listeners of the goals of their revolution. He pledged "equal and exact justice to all men." He affirmed rule by the vote of the majority, but only if "the minority possess their equal rights . . . which law must protect." He emphasized unity and held out a hand of friendship to the Federalists who had opposed him. He promised to "do all the good in my power . . . to the happiness and freedom of all."

Thomas Jefferson moved into the new president's home, which later became known as the White House, on Pennsylvania Avenue. The interior of the building was still under construction, and Jefferson had to work amid the noise of workers with their saws and hammers. Jefferson was used to living in such conditions at Monticello. Most of his time was spent in a small library at the southwest corner of the house.

——————————— ✧ ———————————

When Jefferson lived there, the White House (below)
was called simply the President's House.

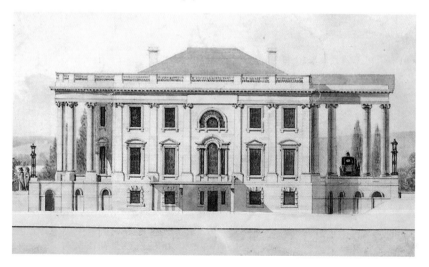

WAR WITH TRIPOLI

The United States fought its first war as a free and independent nation while Thomas Jefferson was president. The war was with the Barbary States, small city-states on the northern coast of Africa, which were home to bands of pirates. These Barbary pirates attacked and robbed merchant ships (ships carrying trade goods) on the high seas and were greatly feared. Many nations, including the United States, paid the pirates money to keep away from their ships.

Thomas Jefferson did not think the United States should pay pirates. In 1801, when Tripoli (one of the Barbary States) demanded more money, President Jefferson refused. On May 14, 1801, the pasha (ruler) of Tripoli declared war on the United States. Jefferson sent U.S. warships commanded by Admiral Edward Preble to blockade the port of Tripoli. The pirates captured one of the American ships, the *Philadelphia*. They dragged off the sailors and jailed them. Then the pirates put their own crew aboard, bragging that they owned an American ship. Under the cover of night, Stephen Decatur, a young American naval officer, sailed a small boat into Tripoli harbor and set the *Philadelphia* on fire. Decatur became a hero for his daring action.

The war with Tripoli went on until 1805, when a U.S. naval captain, William Eaton, invaded Tripoli with a force of five hundred men. They captured the important town of Darnah. The pasha was forced to agree to a peace treaty, and pirates from Tripoli no longer attacked American ships.

Jefferson tried to choose wise and clever men for his cabinet. He picked people from different regions of the country who would represent their home states' points of view. James Madison of Virginia, Jefferson's close friend and the person he trusted most, became secretary of state. Other appointees came from Pennsylvania and the New England states.

Life in the White House was informal under President Jefferson. His clothes were always plain, even when he entertained at state dinners. Once he wore bedroom slippers to receive the British minister. Since Jefferson believed in the equality of all people whatever their position or wealth, meals were served at a round table. That way no seat would be more important than any other. Instead of having guests escorted in to dinner in order of their importance, everyone entered together and took whatever place was available. The food served at the president's round table, however, was not at all simple. Jefferson had a skilled chef who introduced French and Italian foods to the president's house. These foods included pancakes and macaroni, both of which were unfamiliar to most Americans. He also served ice cream made daily from his own recipe.

All people, rich or humble, were welcome to visit the president's house. At a Fourth of July party, the president chatted with diplomats and farmers, senators and clerks. He enjoyed a pleasant conversation with several Native American chiefs and tried to improve his use of the Cherokee language.

One of Jefferson's first acts as president was to pardon everyone who had been jailed under the Alien and Sedition Acts. He sent them personal letters of apology.

Next, he removed the taxes that the government had imposed on U.S. citizens. This included the whiskey tax that had caused a rebellion in Pennsylvania during Washington's administration.

Jefferson was opposed to many federal programs started by Alexander Hamilton, including the national bank. But as president, Jefferson left many in place so as not to cause disunity. On one issue, however, the new president felt strongly. A large national debt had been built up under Hamilton's policies, which favored generous government support of business and commerce. Jefferson had promised to pay off as much of this debt as possible. He managed to do this with the help of Albert Gallatin. This capable secretary of the treasury reduced the national debt from $80 million to $40 million by cutting government expenses sharply, reducing the size of the armed forces, and increasing the income from taxes on imported manufactured goods.

THE LOUISIANA PURCHASE

The greatest accomplishment of Thomas Jefferson's presidency was the Louisiana Purchase. The Louisiana Territory belonged to France. It contained more than one million square miles of forests, plains, mountains, and river valleys stretching from the Mississippi River west and north to the Rocky Mountains. Most of the land was unexplored and unmapped by white Americans, but it included one important port at the mouth of the long Mississippi River. The city of New Orleans was located near the border separating Louisiana from the United States. A French New Orleans could control the

French emperor Napoleon agreed to sell the
Louisiana Territory to the United States in 1803.

Mississippi River and become a threat to the United
States. U.S. leaders feared Napoleon Bonaparte, the ambi-
tious and powerful new ruler of France. In 1803 Jefferson
sent James Monroe to Paris to try to buy New Orleans
from Napoleon for $10 million. Fortunately for the
Americans, Napoleon was in desperate need of money. To
everyone's amazement, he sold the *entire* Louisiana
Territory to the United States for $15 million. In one
move, Thomas Jefferson had doubled the size of the
United States! Americans were thrilled. Celebrations were
held all around the country. Jefferson called the new territory an addition to "the empire of liberty" and a "wide-
spread field for the blessings of liberty."

Many Americans wondered about the vast wilderness.
The president was the most curious of all. He immediately

set to work organizing an expedition to explore the new territory. Jefferson had taught his secretary, Captain Meriwether Lewis, scientific skills such as mapmaking, surveying, and how to identify plants and wildlife. He chose Lewis to lead the expedition together with another experienced soldier, Captain William Clark. They were instructed to travel the Mississippi River to where it joined with the Missouri River and then try to find a water route west to the Pacific Ocean. Lewis and Clark and their crew faced many dangers. Two years later, they returned to Washington, D.C., with important information that would open up the West to settlement.

————————————— ✧ —————————————

*Meriwether Lewis (right) and William Clark (left) led the expedition
to investigate the land bought in the Louisiana Purchase.*

THE LEWIS AND CLARK EXPEDITION

With the Louisiana Purchase, the United States gained a huge new parcel of land. There were many legends about this mysterious territory. Stories were told about mountains of salt and seven-foot-tall beavers. President Jefferson sent Meriwether Lewis and William Clark and a team of men they called the Corps of Discovery to explore the territory. Jefferson instructed Lewis and Clark to survey the land and keep a scientific record of plants, animals, rivers, and mountains they saw. He wanted them to observe the people who lived there and write down details of their languages and customs. But the main goal was to find a water route to the Pacific Ocean—a northwest passage.

The Corps of Discovery set out from St. Louis, Missouri, on May 21, 1804. The team of forty-eight men included hunters, soldiers, and boatmen. They traveled up the Missouri River on a keelboat (large riverboat) and several small boats. After covering 1,400 miles, they were forced by icy-cold weather to stop in present-day North Dakota and spend the winter with Mandans, a Native American tribe.

❖

Clark kept careful records of the expedition in this elk-skin journal.

The following spring, they set off again up the Missouri River into Montana. A French Canadian trapper named Charbonneau and his Shoshone wife, Sacagawea, joined the group. Sacagawea was of great help to the expedition. With her small child strapped to her back, she guided them through dangerous territory. At one point, when they were out of food and supplies, Sacagawea persuaded a group of Shoshone Indians to help the explorers.

Lewis and Clark found that there was no water passage from the Mississippi River to the Pacific. Instead, they had to trudge through deep snow on narrow trails. Sacagawea's Shoshone friends gave them horses to cross the Rocky Mountains. On the other side of the mountains, they paddled down the Columbia River. On November 15, 1805, the explorers sighted the Pacific Ocean. They spent the winter on the coast and in spring began the return journey.

In spite of dangers and hardships, the Corps of Discovery completed its mission. They recorded 122 animals and 178 plants and trees that were new to them. They wrote of seeing bison, elk, deer, and a creature they called a "cabic" (pronghorn, an animal that resembles an antelope). They described how Captain Clark killed an enormous brown bear almost nine feet tall. The explorers of the Corps of Discovery were the first white people ever to see grizzly bears. Their records describe prairie dogs that lived in villages of their own and black-footed ferrets that also roamed the prairies.

Lewis and Clark were welcomed as heroes when they returned. They had not found a water route to the Pacific, but they had mapped and opened up the American West for future pioneers and settlers.

Jefferson ran for reelection in 1804. He was the most popular man in the country and won his second presidential election in a landslide. This time, Aaron Burr was not a candidate. He and Alexander Hamilton had long been bitter enemies. Burr killed Hamilton in a duel that shocked the nation. He fled to the Louisiana Territory, where he plotted to establish a new government. He was arrested and tried for treason. Though his guilt could not be proven, many people considered Burr a traitor, and he went to live abroad. Jefferson's new choice for vice president was George Clinton, governor of New York.

THE SECOND TERM

Just before his second presidential election, in April 1804, Jefferson rushed home to Monticello to see his twenty-five-year-old daughter, Maria, who had been ill following childbirth. He arrived just in time to hold her in his arms once more before she died. It seemed as though tragedy and grief would forever haunt the Jefferson family. "My loss is great," Thomas Jefferson wrote sadly to a friend. "I have lost even the half of all I had."

Jefferson's second term as president was less successful than the first. He faced many challenges, old and new. Several years earlier, a man named James Callender had asked Jefferson to get him an appointment as postmaster of Richmond. Jefferson had refused. Callender never forgave him and determined to gain revenge. In a series of articles, he accused Jefferson of being the father of children who had been born to one of his slaves, Sally Hemings. Jefferson would not dignify the slander by answering it publicly. In private, however, he told friends that it was not true. (Modern

Burr and Hamilton chose pistols as their dueling weapons.
Hamilton died the day after being wounded by Burr's bullet.

─────────────── ✧ ───────────────

DNA evidence shows that one of the Hemings family ancestors was indeed a member of the Jefferson family. Some people think it was a Jefferson nephew who fathered the child.
Some believe it was Thomas Jefferson himself.)

Critics also raged at Jefferson about his conduct in foreign
affairs. The British, who were at war with France, were board-
ing U.S. ships at sea. They forced American sailors into service with the British navy. Jefferson wanted to avoid war, so
he declared a trade embargo against Great Britain. This meant
that Americans could no longer trade with the British.
Jefferson thought this would hurt Britain, but it hurt U.S.
businesses more. Business owners turned against the president.
Articles and cartoons attacking him appeared in newspapers

This cartoon from the early 1800s shows that many Americans, especially merchants, were bitter about the trade embargo imposed on Britain.

———————— ◇ ————————

all over the country. Finally, Jefferson gave in to the pressure and stopped the embargo. It had been a failure.

By the time his second term was up in 1809, Thomas Jefferson was relieved to be leaving public life. "Never did a prisoner, released from his chains, feel such relief as I shall on shaking off the shackles of power." Jefferson's party wanted him to run again, but he decided it was best to follow George Washington's example and step down after two terms. He looked forward to returning to the one place where he could be happy—Monticello.

CHAPTER ELEVEN

THE FINAL YEARS

"You ask if I would agree to live
my... seventy-three years over again....
Yea. I think, with you, that it is a
good world, on the whole."
—Thomas Jefferson to John Adams, 1816

For much of his life, duty to his country had called Thomas Jefferson away from Monticello. "Nature intended me for the tranquil pursuits of science," he wrote. "But the enormities of the times in which I have lived have forced me to take a part." At sixty-five, he could look forward to spending the rest of his days at his beloved home in "tranquil pursuits."

His first task was to complete Monticello. Jefferson planned the final details, including horseback-riding trails, orchards, and gardens. He chose paint colors and draperies and the placement of paintings, maps, and other objects. He treasured the time he had to read and study—there were still many things he wanted to learn. His library grew to an enormous size. Jefferson later sold the books to the federal government, and they became part of the collection at the Library of Congress.

The "sage of Monticello" wrote to people in every walk of life. He exchanged letters with the new president, James Madison, and other government leaders who sought his advice. He began a correspondence with his old friend, John Adams. They had been estranged for many years. They wrote to each other regularly. Their letters were filled with discussions on politics, philosophy, religion, and many other subjects.

————————— ◇ —————————

The Library of Congress houses more than 126 million items on more than 500 miles of bookshelves.

Jefferson corresponded daily with family, friends, and interesting people around the world. During his lifetime, he wrote nearly twenty thousand letters. In one note, he offered advice to the young son of a friend. These are his ten commandments for daily living:

1. *Never put off till tomorrow what you can do today.*
2. *Never trouble another for what you can do yourself.*
3. *Never spend your money before you have it.*
4. *Never buy what you do not want because it is cheap; it will be dear to you.*
5. *Pride costs us more than hunger, thirst, and cold.*
6. *We never repent of having eaten too little.*
7. *Nothing is troublesome that we do willingly.*
8. *How much pain have cost us the evils which have never happened.*
9. *Take things always by their smooth handle.*
10. *When angry, count ten before you speak; if very angry, a hundred.*

Jefferson wrote in a small office that he called his "cabinet." It contained his own inventions for a comfortable workspace: revolving bookstand, table and chair, and his polygraph machine. He always worked at set hours each day. Everyone knew he must not be disturbed during this time.

Jefferson's daughter Martha lived at Monticello and supervised the household. The home was always filled with those he loved—children, grandchildren, nieces, nephews, and other family members. They gathered in the evenings for games and music. Sometimes Jefferson would play the violin while his grandchildren danced around him. Many evenings were devoted to books. The children were expected to follow their grandfather's example and read quietly. One of his granddaughters later remembered, "He talked with us affectionately...our small follies he treated with good humor...our graver ones with kind...admonition....I used to...sit on his knee and play with his watch chain. I loved and honored him above all earthly beings."

A constant flow of visitors came to Monticello. It was not unusual for twenty or more guests to be present at breakfast. They were served tea, coffee, muffins, ham, and warm corn bread. People came from all over the world. They toured Monticello, exclaiming over its charm and beauty. They watched in amazement as Jefferson demonstrated his inventions. They discussed the latest news of the country and the world.

Thomas Jefferson still believed that free public education was important to a democratic society. He spent years developing his concepts for an ideal public university. He set out the courses, types of faculty, student preparation, and classroom design. He drew up architectural plans for a building that would embody his educational goals. In 1825 Jefferson's dream came true when the University of Virginia opened its doors. It was not just a college for the wealthy. Poor students who showed talent were admitted free.

Thomas Jefferson lived to see the fiftieth anniversary of his beloved country. He died at Monticello on July 4, 1826,

Independence Day, at age 83. His friend and fellow patriot, John Adams, died on the same day. Jefferson's daughter Martha found a poem her father had written for her.

Then farewell, my dear, my loved daughter, adieu!
The last pang of life is in parting from you.

Jefferson had prepared an inscription for his gravestone. It listed what he considered his most important achievements.

Here was buried Thomas Jefferson
author of the
Declaration of American Independence
of the Statute of Virginia for Religious Freedom
and Father of the
University of Virginia.

THE JEFFERSON MEMORIAL

In 1934 Congress authorized a national monument to honor
the third president of the United States. The Thomas Jefferson
Memorial (above) was begun in 1938 and completed in 1943.
It is located in East Potomac Park in Washington, D.C.

John Russell Pope designed the Roman-style white marble
building to honor Jefferson's love of classical architecture.
Twenty-six graceful columns form a circle covered by a domed
ceiling. The visitor climbs a broad flight of steps to view a bronze
statue of Jefferson, which is nineteen feet high and stands upon
a black pedestal. A circular panel below the dome bears
Jefferson's words: "I have sworn upon the altar of God eternal
hostility against every form of tyranny over the mind of man."

Other quotations are engraved on the marble panels.
These words about freedom and democracy reflect the basic

ideas upon which the United States and all democracies have been built. Here are some of the monument's engraved quotations from the Declaration of Independence:

"We hold these truths to be self-evident: that all men are created equal, that they are endowed by their Creator with certain inalienable rights, among these are life, liberty, and the pursuit of happiness."

"We . . . solemnly publish and declare, that these colonies are and of right ought to be free and independent states."

The rest of the quotations in the memorial are from Jefferson's various writings. Here are a few of them:

"No man shall be compelled to . . . support any religious worship . . . or shall otherwise suffer on account of his religious . . . belief."

"God who gave us life gave us liberty."

"Establish the law for educating the common people."

"Nothing is more certainly written in the book of fate than that these people [slaves] are to be free."

"Laws and institutions must go hand in hand with the progress of the human mind. . . . As new discoveries are made, new truths discovered . . . institutions must advance also to keep pace with the times."

Timeline

1743 Thomas Jefferson is born at the Shadwell estate in Virginia.

1757 His father, Peter Jefferson, dies.

1760 Jefferson attends the College of William and Mary in Williamsburg, Virginia.

1762 Jefferson begins to study law with George Wythe.

1767 Jefferson is admitted to practice law.

1768 Jefferson is elected to the House of Burgesses in Virginia. He begins building Monticello.

1770 Shadwell burns down.

1771 Jefferson moves to a cottage at Monticello.

1772 Jefferson marries Martha Wayles Skelton. Their daughter Martha (Patsy) is born.

1774 Jefferson writes *A Summary View of the Rights of British America*. A daughter, Jane Randolph, is born.

1775 Jefferson is elected to the Continental Congress. His daughter Jane Randolph dies.

1776 Jefferson writes a draft of the Declaration of Independence. His mother, Jane Randolph Jefferson, dies. Jefferson is elected to Virginia House of Delegates and drafts Virginia Statute for Religious Freedom.

1777 An unnamed son is born and dies.

1778 Another daughter, Mary (also called Maria or Polly), is born.

1779	Jefferson is elected governor of Virginia.
1780	His daughter Lucy Elizabeth is born.
1781	Lucy Elizabeth dies.
1782	Jefferson writes *Notes on the State of Virginia.* Another daughter, also named Lucy Elizabeth, is born. Wife Martha dies.
1783	Jefferson is elected a delegate to Congress.
1784	Jefferson serves in France as commissioner and then minister. Daughter Lucy Elizabeth dies.
1787	*Notes on the State of Virginia* is published.
1790	Jefferson serves as first U.S. secretary of state.
1797	Jefferson is elected vice president of the United States.
1801	Jefferson is elected third president of the United States.
1803	Jefferson approves purchase of the Louisiana Territory from France.
1804	Jefferson sends out Lewis and Clark expedition. Daughter Maria Jefferson Eppes dies.
1806	Lewis and Clark expedition returns.
1809	Jefferson retires from presidency and public life. Remodeling of Monticello is mostly completed.
1817	Jefferson designs and lays cornerstone for University of Virginia.
1825	University of Virginia opens.
1826	Jefferson dies at Monticello on July 4.

SOURCE NOTES

9 Sarah N. Randolph, *The Domestic Life of Thomas Jefferson* (Cambridge, MA: University Press, 1947), 4.

10 Ibid., 8.

13 E. M. Betts and J. A. Bear Jr., eds., *The Family Letters of Thomas Jefferson* (New York: Columbia University Press, 1966), 470.

14 Russell Shorto, *Thomas Jefferson and the American Ideal,* (Hauppauge, NY: Barrons Juvenile, 1987), 17.

16 Fawn M. Brodie, *Thomas Jefferson, An Intimate History* (New York: W. W. Norton, 1974), 39.

18 Claude G. Bowers, *The Young Jefferson* (Boston: Houghton Mifflin, 1969), 14.

20 Randolph, 12.

20 Ibid.

21 Ibid.

21 Ibid., 13.

21 Ibid., 12.

21 Bowers, 21.

21 Randolph, 10.

23 Randolph, 23.

24 Bowers, 29.

26 Brodie, 69.

26 Ibid., 70.

26 Ibid.

27 Ibid., 72.

27 Ibid.

27 Ibid.

31 Ibid., 81.

31 Bowers, 45.

33 Brodie, 89.

33 Bowers, 47.

33 Ibid.

35 E. M. Halliday, *Understanding Thomas Jefferson* (New York: HarperCollins, 2001), 32.

35 Brodie, 86.

36 Jack McLaughlin, *Jefferson and Monticello* (New York: Henry Holt & Co., 1988), 217.

38 Bowers, 49.

39 Randolph, 28.

40 Dumas Malone, *Jefferson the Virginian* (Boston: Little Brown, & Co., 1948), 188.

42 A. J. Langguth, *Patriots: The Men Who Started the American Revolution* (New York: Touchstone/Simon & Schuster, 1988), 69.

42 Bowers, 41.

44 Ibid., 88.

45 Malone, 186.

46 Langguth, 223.

47 *Encyclopaedia Britannica*, 14th ed., s.v. "Declaration of Independence."

49 Brodie, 108–109.

50 Ibid., 107.

50 Ibid., 111.

51 Randolph, 30.

51 Brodie, 115.

52 Bowers, 148.

52 *Encyclopaedia Britannica*, 14th ed., s.v. "Declaration of Independence."

52 Ibid.

53 Langguth, 307.

55 American Heritage Publishing, *Thomas Jefferson and His World* (New York: American Heritage Publishing, 1960), 53.

56 Bowers, 212.

57 Randolph, 35.

60 Ibid.

62 Brodie, 149.

62 Ibid., 161

62 Ibid., 157.

63 Ibid., 152.

63 Ibid., 153.

64 Randolph, 40.

65 Ibid., 41–42.

65 Ibid.
65 Bowers, 311.
65 Randolph, 42.
66 Willard Sterne Randall, *Thomas Jefferson: A Life* (New York: Henry Holt & Co., 1993), 385.
66 Roger Bruns, *Thomas Jefferson* (New York: Chelsea House Publishers,1986), 51.
68 Randolph, 44.
70 Page Smith, *John Adams* (New York: Doubleday, 1962), 625.
73 *Encarta Encyclopedia*, s.v. "Thomas Jefferson." (Redmond, WA: Microsoft Corporation, 1999), CD-ROM.
75 Jefferson to John Adams, letter, 1819, *Favorite Jefferson Quotes*, <http://etext.virginia.edu/ jefferson/quotations/jeffl.htm>
76 Randolph, 116.
76 Ibid., 496.
77 Brodie, 253.
77 Jefferson to William Short, letter, 1825, *Favorite Jefferson Quotes*, <http://etext.virginia.edu/ jefferson/quotations/jeffl.htm>
77 *Encarta Encyclopedia*, s.v. "Thomas Jefferson." (Redmond, WA: Microsoft Corporation, 1999), CD-ROM.
80 Brodie, 263.
85 Randall, 548.
85 Ibid., 547.
86 Ibid., 548.
86 Ibid.
86 Randolph, 235.
90 Randall, 567.
94 Randolph, 257.
96 Ibid., 278.
97 Randolph, 311.
97 William J. Bennett, *Our Sacred Honor* (New York: Simon & Schuster, 1997), 222.
99 Randolph, 278.

100 Ibid., 295.
101 Ibid., 370.
101 Randall, 595.

BIBLIOGRAPHY

American Heritage Publishing. *Thomas Jefferson and His World*. New York: American Heritage Publishing, 1960.

Bennett, William J. *Our Sacred Honor*. New York: Simon & Schuster, 1997.

Bowers, Claude G. *The Young Jefferson*. Boston: Houghton Mifflin, 1969.

Brodie, Fawn M. *Thomas Jefferson, an Intimate History*. New York: W. W. Norton, 1974.

Bruns, Roger. *Thomas Jefferson*. New York: Chelsea House Publishers, 1986.

The Columbia World of Quotations. New York: Columbia University Press, 1966.

Ellis, Joseph J. *Founding Brothers*. New York: Alfred A. Knopf, 2000.

Fleming, Thomas. *The Man from Monticello: An Intimate Life of Thomas Jefferson*. New York: William Morrow & Co., 1969.

Halliday, E. M. *Understanding Thomas Jefferson*. New York: HarperCollins, 2001.

Langguth, A. J. *Patriots: The Men Who Started the American Revolution*. New York: Touchstone / Simon & Schuster, 1988.

Malone, Dumas. *Jefferson the Virginian*. Boston: Little Brown, & Co., 1948.

McLaughlin, Jack. *Jefferson and Monticello*. New York: Henry Holt & Co., 1988.

Randall, Willard Sterne. *Thomas Jefferson: A Life*. New York: Henry Holt & Co., 1993.

Randolph, Sarah N. *The Domestic Life of Thomas Jefferson*. Cambridge, MA: University Press, 1947.

Shorto, Russell. *Thomas Jefferson and the American Ideal*. Hauppauge, NY: Barrons Juvenile, 1987.

Smith, Page. *John Adams*. New York: Doubleday, 1962.

FURTHER READING AND WEBSITES

Aldridge, Rebecca. *Thomas Jefferson.* Mankato, MN: Bridgestone Books 2001.

Bober, Natalie S. *Thomas Jefferson: Man on a Mountain.* New York: Atheneum, 1999.

Ferris, Jeri Chase. *Thomas Jefferson: Father of Liberty.* Minneapolis: Carolrhoda Books, Inc., 1998.

Fisher, Leonard Everett. *Monticello.* New York: Holiday House, 1988.

Hakim, Jay. *From Colonies to Country.* New York: Oxford University Press, 1999.

Meltzer, Milton. *Thomas Jefferson: The Revolutionary Aristocrat.* Danbury, CT: Franklin Watts, 1991.

Monsell, Helen Albee. *Thomas Jefferson: The Third President of the U.S.* New York: Simon & Schuster, 1999.

Monticello: The Home of Thomas Jefferson. <http://www.monticello.org>. This site has information about Jefferson and virtual tours of the house and gardens.

Shanger, Rosalyn. *How We Crossed the West: The Adventures of Lewis and Clark.* Washington, D.C.: National Geographic, 1997.

Sherrow, Victoria. *Thomas Jefferson.* Minneapolis: Lerner Publications Company, 2002.

Stein, R. Conrad. *The Declaration of Independence.* Danbury, CT: Children's Press, 1995.

Thomas Jefferson Digital Archive. <http://etext.virginia.edu/jefferson/>. Collected by the University of Virginia, this site offers Jefferson papers, an early biography of him, selected quotations, and the history of Jefferson's plans for the University of Virginia.

Young, Robert. *A Personal Tour of Monticello.* Minneapolis: Lerner Publications Company, 1999.

INDEX

death, 100–101; Declaration of Independence, 6, 7–8, 52–53, 101; diplomat, 67, 68–74; farming, 13–14, 20, 25, 27, 30, 38, 50, 56, 77, 81; in France, 68–74; governor, 57, 60–61; habits, 21–22, 24–25, 81, 88, 99; health, 46, 51, 61–62, 76–77; inventions, 20, 36, 72, 81, 99, 100; and law, 23–25, 27–30, 29–30, 38, 56, 73, 83, 103; love of books, 14, 17, 18, 31, 70, 98; marriage, 34–35, 64–65; music, 17, 18, 25, 33–34, 64, 99; Native Americans, 10, 62, 88; Paris, 68–74; personality, 13, 19–20, 24; philosophy of, 29, 56, 62, 76, 77, 83, 84, 85–86, 88, 99; president, 85–91, 94–96; secretary of state, 76–80; slavery, 29–30, 38, 52–53, 56, 62, 94–95; vice president, 82–83; writings of, 22, 24–25, 30, 52–53, 62–64, 67–68, 70, 79, 82, 98–99, 102–103

Lafayette, Marquis de, 69–70, 73–74
Lewis and Clark, 91–93
Library of Congress, 98
Louisiana Purchase, 89–90, 91

Madison, James, 73, 82, 88
Maury, Joseph, 17, 18
Monroe, James, 90
Monticello, 34–35, 36–37, 50, 55, 61, 75, 80, 81, 83; British capture, 59–60; retirement at, 97–100; Jefferson designs, 27, 28, 32–33, 36

Native Americans, 10, 62, 88, 93
Notes on the State of Virginia, 62–64

Paine, Thomas, 51–52
Parliament, British, 40–41, 42, 43, 45–46
Patriots, 44, 48, 51, 52

political parties, 79, 80

Randolph, William, 11; family of, 11–13
religion, 56, 62, 101
rivers, 9–10, 92; Mississippi, 89, 91, 93

Sacagawea, 93
Shadwell, 9, 11, 12, 13, 14, 17–18, 22, 25; fire at, 31–32
slaves and slavery, 9, 13, 28–30, 38, 51, 52–53, 59–60, 94; Jefferson's views on, 29, 30, 52, 62
Small, William, 20, 25
Sons of Liberty, 43

taxation, 89; Stamp Act, 40–43; on tea, 44–45; Townshend Act, 43; on whiskey, 80–81, 89
Thomas Jefferson Memorial, 102–103
Tripoli, war with, 87
Tyler, John, 22, 23, 25

United States: Bank of, 78, 89; Constitution of, 73, 78; debts of, 71, 77–78, 89; expansion of, 89–93; foreign relations of, 78–79, 82, 87, 95–96; formation of, 52–53, 68, 77–78; navy of, 87, 95; Senate of, 82
University of Virginia, 100, 101

Virginia, 9, 10, 50–51, 55, 56, 57–59, 60–61; Jefferson writes about, 62–64
Ordinance for Religious Freedom, 56

Washington, D.C., 78, 85
Washington, George, 43, 83; as general, 49–50, 53–55, 58; as president, 75–76, 79, 80, 81, 96
Whiskey Rebellion, 80–81
White House, 86, 88
William and Mary College, 18–19, 22, 23
Wythe, George, 21, 23–24

ABOUT THE AUTHOR

Carol H. Behrman was born in Brooklyn, New York, graduated from City College of New York, and attended Columbia University's Teachers' College, where she majored in education. For many years, Behrman taught grades five through eight at the Glen Ridge Middle School in New Jersey. She has written twenty books, fiction and nonfiction, for children and young adults, as well as seven writing textbooks. Her previous biographies include *Fiddler to the World: The Inspiring Life of Itzhak Perlman, Roberto Clemente, Andrew Jackson, John Adams*, and *Miss Dr. Lucy*, the story of the first woman dentist in America. Behrman lives in Sarasota, Florida.

PHOTO ACKNOWLEDGMENTS

The images in this book are used with the permission of: © North Wind Picture Archives, pp. 2, 6, 19, 41, 42, 43, 54, 55, 58, 59, 69, 77, 81, 91 (left and right), 92; Laura Westlund, p. 11; Monticello/Thomas Jefferson Memorial Foundation, pp. 12, 35, 96; Peter Newark's American Pictures, pp. 13, 53; Independent Picture Service, pp. 17, 49 (left), 90; Library of Congress, pp. 20 (LC-MSS-27748-64), 21, 24 (Thomas Jefferson Papers Series 5. Commonplace Books), 36 (LC-H812-T-M09-007-A), 45 (LC-USZ62-9), 46 (LC-USZ62-3775), 48 (LC-D4-12943), 63 (Thomas Jefferson Papers Series 1. General Correspondence, 1651-1827), 73 (LC-USZ62-106), 74 (LC-USZ62-10833), 82 (Thomas Jefferson Papers Series 7. Miscellaneous Bound Volumes), 86 (LC-USZ62-3068), 95 (LC-USZ62-75928), 98 (HABS,DC,WASH,461A-26), 102 (LC-USE6-D-010109); Massachusetts Historical Society, pp. 28, 32; Tom Costa, "Virginia Runaways" http://www.uvawise.edu/history/runaways, p. 29; National Archives, p. 49 (right); Architect of the Capitol, p. 61; The Art Archive/Musée Carnavalet Paris/Dagli Orti (A), p. 71; © Buddy Mays/Travel Stock, p. 72; Independence National Historical Park, p. 84.

Front Cover: © Bettmann/CORBIS.